FIFTH GENERATION COMPUTERS

FIFTH GENERATION COMPUTERS

Compiled and Edited by
RICHARD K. MILLER, CMfgE

Published by
THE FAIRMONT PRESS, INC.
700 Indian Trail
Lilburn, GA 30247

Library of Congress Data: LCC: 86-45549
Miller, R.K.
Fifth Generation Computers.

ISBN 0-88173-050-5

Published by The Fairmont Press, Inc.
700 Indian Trail, NW
Lilburn, GA 30247

ISBN 0-88173-050-5 FP
ISBN 0-13-314295-7 PH

Printed in the United States of America.

Distributed by Prentice-Hall, Inc.
A division of Simon & Schuster
Englewood Cliffs, NJ 07632

Prentice-Hall International (UK) Limited, *London*
Prentice-Hall of Australia Pty. Limited, *Sydney*
Editora Prentice-Hall do Brasil, Ltda., *Rio de Janeiro*
Prentice-Hall Canada Inc., *Toronto*
Prentice-Hall Hispanoamericana, S.A., *Mexico*
Prentice-Hall of India Private Limited, *New Delhi*
Prentice-Hall of Japan, Inc., *Tokyo*
Prentice-Hall of Southeast Asia Pte. Ltd., *Singapore*

TABLE OF CONTENTS

1

Executive Summary

The commitment to develop Fifth Generation computers is strong in the United States and Japan. Fifth Generation research aims at producing an entirely new breed of computers based on symbolic inference and using parallel processing for fast processing huge amounts of data. Previous generation computer classifications are: (1) vacuum tubes, (2) transistors, (3) integrated circuits, and (4) large-scale integration chips. The Fifth Generation computers will use advanced forms of VLSI technology and new superchips.

The idea of Fifth Generation computers was sprung on the world in 1982 by the Japanese. Their Ministry of International Trade and Industry (MITI) announced an ambitious 10-year research program (with government funding of $500 million US dollars) aimed at developing a new generation of computing technology for the creation of machines that make logical inferences, deal effectively with masses of information, use speech and images to interact with humans, and perform many tasks previously thought to require human expertise. The launching of the Japanese research program was preceded by three years of study within MITI; the research project itself is staffed by a core of government scientists augmented by researchers selected from Japanese industry.

There are eight major research projects aimed at developing fifth generation computers, advanced microelectronics, new man-machine interfaces or advanced applications. These projects are summarized below.

ICOT/Institute for New Generation Computer Technology

In 1982, Japan's Ministry of International Trade and Industry announced a 10 year, $500 million Fifth Generation project. The project, being carried out by the Institute for New Generation Computer Technology will incorporate AI concepts, and has as objectives to develop a machine which will:

- Listen when spoken to, then do what it is told.
- Help program itself.
- Sort through volumes of facts to find and use only what is pertinent.
- Make logical inferences.
- Translate foreign languages.
- Treat images and graphics the same as words ("see" and "understand" a photo, for example).
- Learn from its own experience.
- Designed for both portable and fixed-based systems.

MCC/Microelectronics and Computer Technology Cooperative

A major Fifth Generation project is being carried out by the Microelectronics and Computer Technology Cooperative, based in Austin, Texas. Incorporated in August 1982, MCC includes 19 major U.S. corporations. The organization's first projects are:

- The development of new computer architectures for the Alpha-Omega computer; applicable to AI and database media ($15 million annually for 10 years).

- Software technology (creating tools for programmers to lower software costs) for program development that operates on the Alpha-Omega computer ($8 million annually for 8 years).

- Computer-aided design and manufacturing for the production of VLSI chips ($11 million annually for 8 years).

- Component packaging, to solve increased need for pin connections in VLSI chips ($5 million annually for 6 years).

SRC/Semiconductor Research Corporation

The North Carolina-based Semiconductor Research Corporation is funded by twelve major U.S. corporations. SRC works through 30 U.S. universities. Over the next two years, $40 million will be directed to finance individual university research. One objective of the SRC is the development of a 4 megabyte chip by 1987. They believe that this would put them three years ahead of Japan. A 16-megabyte chip would be their next goal. Major project areas are:

- Microstructure sciences: materials and device fabrication technologies

- Design sciences: design automation and system-component interactions

- Manufacturing systems: automation, robotics, simulation, packaging and testing

DARPA/The Defense Advanced Research Projects Agency

Another major U.S. effort is the Strategic Computing and Survivability Project, known as Supercomputer. The Defense Advanced Research Projects Agency intends to spend $500 million over 5 years in the development of a super computer for defense and civilian applications. The budget was $50 million for 1984, and $95 million for 1985. Areas of research include:

artificial intelligence, software development, computer architectures, an autonomous land vehicle, expert systems for aircraft, and fleet command centers.

ESPRIT/European Strategic Program of Research and Development in Information Technology

ESPRIT is a European giant computer development effort, organized by EEC, who will contribute half of the $1.5 billion budget. Japan's government, on the other hand, has committed only $50 million for the first three years of its program. ESPRIT's project areas are: advanced microelectronics, software technology, advanced information processing, office systems and computer integrated manufacturing.

Alvey

In Great Britian, the Alvey Program for Advanced Information Technology has a 5 year funding level of 350 Pounds British Sterling. Research will be conducted in microelectronics, software engineering, knowledge-based systems, and man-machine interfaces.

CAM-I/Computer Aided Manufacturing-International

Computer Aided Manufacturing-International, Arlington, Texas, is a nonprofit membership organization engaged in research and development of computer-aided manufacturing technology. CAM-I was formed in 1972 to further the cooperative research and development (R&D) efforts of companies with common interests in computer-aided design and manufacturing (CAD/CAM). The corporation is member-owned and supported by industrial, governmental and educational organizations in Australia, Europe, Japan, and North and South America. Project areas include geometric modeling, process planning, CAD/CAM, computer-aided quality assurance and robotics.

SDF/The System Development Foundation

The System Development Foundation, a California nonprofit corporation, was organized by the Rand Corporation in 1956. Annual funding is about $37 million in the areas of robotics, information science, man-machine interface, and non-von Neumann computation.

2

Comparison of Fifth Generation Projects

The eight fifth generation and advanced computer projects can be compared on several levels:

a. Goals and objectives
b. Funding arrangements
c. Research budgets
d. Research performance
e. Availability of research results

This chapter presents an analysis of the projects with respect to these five areas.

Goals and Objectives

The stated goals of the eight projects are:

ICOT: Market leadership
MCC: Market dominance
SRC: Semiconductor industry support
DARPA: National security
ESPRIT: Improve competitiveness
ALVEY: Improve competitiveness
CAM-I: Further cooperative R&D in CAD/CAM
SRF: Provide grants for U.S. university research

The project objectives are:

ICOT (Institute for New Generation Computer Technology)

- Hardware architecture and software to achieve inference function.
- Hardware architecture and software to achieve knowledge base function.
- Hardware architecture and software to achieve intelligent interface function.
- Software to achieve intelligent programming.

MCC (Microelectronics and Computer Technology Corporation)

- The development of new computer architectures for the Alpha-Omega computer; applicable to AI and database media.
- Software technology (creating tools for programmers to lower software costs) for program development that operates on the Alpha-Omega computer.
- Computer-aided design and manufacturing for the production of VLSI chips.

- Component packaging, to solve increased need for pin connections in VLSI chips.

(SRC) Semiconductor Research Corporation)

- Microstructure sciences: materials and device fabrication technologies.
- Design sciences: design automation and system-component interactions.
- Manufacturing systems: automation, robotics, simulation, packaging and testing.

(DARPA) Defense Advanced Research Projects Agency)

- Artificial intelligence.
- Software development.
- Computer architectures.
- Autonomous land vehicle.
- Expert systems for aircraft.
- Fleet command center.

ESPRIT (European Strategic Program on Research in Information Technology

- Advanced microelectronics.
- Software technology.
- Advanced information processing.
- Office systems.
- Computer integrated manufacturing

Alvey Program for Advanced Information Technology

- Software engineering, the efficient specification and generation of the instructions for the machines.

- The interface between man and machine

- The study of intelligent knowledge based systems (IKBS).

- Advanced in very large scale integration (VLSI) of circuits on silicon.

CAM-I (Computer Aided Manufacturing-International, Inc.)

- Framework project
- Geometric modeling project
- Process planning program
- Advanced N/C project
- Sculptured surfaces project
- Factory management project
- Electronics automation program
- Computer aided quality assurance
- Robotics software project

SDF (System Development Foundation)

- Robotics (perception, locomotion, motor control).
- Computer music.
- The neurosciences.
- Principles of information science.
- Computational linguistics and speech.
- The man-machine interface.
- Non-von Neumann computation.
- Symbolic mathematics.

Funding Arrangements

The Microelectronic and Computer Technology Corporation (MCC), Semiconductor Research Cooperative (SRC), and Computer Aided Manufacturing-International, Inc. (CAM-I) projects are completely financed by member corporations.

The Defense Advanced Research Projects Agency (DARPA) project is completely financed by the United States Government.

The sale of System Development Foundation (SDF) to Burroughs Corporation in 1981 provided funds to conduct current grant-making activities.

Research Budgets

The research funding levels of the advanced computer projects provide a measure of impact which they may be expected to produce.

The Ministry of International Trade and Industry (MITI) has budgeted 100 billion yen (about $415 million at the current exchange rate) over a 10 year period. The first three-year phase allots $40 million for basic research and will be funded entirely by MITI. After this initial phase, heavy budgeting is planned for the years of expensive developmental engineering. The 1984 budget was $21.2 million, nearly double the previous year.

In the start-up phases of MCC, the following approximate budgets are estimated:

1982: $ 5 million
1983: $11 million
1984: $15 million
1985: $30 million

As the program develops, a $150 million annual budget is projected.

The Strategic Computer Initiative of DARPA has expected budgets of $600 million over the next five years and more than $1 billion during the next 10 years. Current funding levels are $50 million for fiscal year 1984, $95 million for 1985, and $150 million for 1986 for research in AI, software, and computer architecture. Over the past 20 years, DARPA has invested more than $500 million in computer research. The following budgets are projected for the current DARPA project:

$50 million: FY84
$75 million: FY85
$150-200 million: future years

ESPRIT has a committed funding of $11.5 million and planned funding of up to $1.5 billion over five years.

The Alvey Program for Advanced Information Technology will have finances of 350 million Pounds British Sterling over a five year period.

Grants approved by the System Development Foundation for the period from May 1981 to June 1983 total $36,879,364, with the following categorical allocations:

Principles of information science	$ 5,346,431
Computational linguistics and speech	3,696,682
Symbolic mathematics	611,304
Robotics: perception, locomotion and motor control	$ 9,158,385
Non-von Neumann computation	2,269,847
The neurosciences	5,930,671
The man-machine interface	2,622,340
Computer music	7,193,704

Research Performance

The Microelectronics and Computer Technology Corporation (MCC) is the only one of the eight projects which performs research in-house. The other seven projects provide management and funding for research which is contracted to university, corporate, and/or government laboratories.

Research Results

The research results of the ICOT, MCC, ESPRIT and ALVEY projects are available only to member corporations. The projects have various provisions for licensing results or otherwise making their findings publicly available.

Research results of CAM-I and SDF are in the public domain.

Research results of the DARPA project are the exclusive property of the U.S. Department of Defense, however much of this information is expected to trickle down to U.S. industry.

3

The Impact of Fifth Generation Computers

Since the announcement of the ICOT project to develop Fifth Generation computers by the Japanese Ministry of International Trade and Industry in 1982, there has been much concern regarding the impact that a new generation of computers may have on society. Recognizing the influence of computer technology on today's society, it is clear that a second computer revolution would have the potential of altering the balance of international power as well as influencing the life style of virtually every individual in the industrialized world. Some of the areas of impact are:

- Science/Engineering: Computer-aided design, computer-aided engineering, database access
- Office: Voice database
- Industry: Robotics, system configuration, simulation
- Software: Debugging aides, development tools, language specifications
- Military: Command, communication, and control cryptography, missile guidance
- Aerospace: Traffic control, space exploration, weapons systems
- Health: Diagnostics, prosthesis, automated lab tests
- Service/Home: Insurance planning, banking, electronic shopping
- Education: Learning aides, automated libraries, learning theory
- Quality of Life: Games, computer aided tools, electronic libraries

The potential impact of the Fifth Generation computers is most evident by the multibillion dollar, worldwide response to the Japanese ICOT project. In the United States, the launching of three major programs has been seen. The DARPA (Defense Advanced Research Projects Agency) Strategic Computing Program seeks to maintain U.S. world superiority in Fifth Generation Systems for both military and commercial purposes. DARPA plans to spend about $1 billion over the next six years to develop "intelligent" computing systems able, for example, to guide unmanned tanks and to assist military pilots. The money will be spent in U.S. universities and industry to advance the technologies which underly Fifth Generation computing: microelectronics, computer architecture, software engineering and artificial intelligence.

Also in the U.S., MCC was formed as a cooperative venture by several of the major computer and microelectronics firms to do advanced, long-term research in Fifth Generation technologies, while SRC is a similar venture focusing on microelectronics.

In the UK, the Alvey program has provided funding of a similar level and scope to the Japanese, for research in microelectronics, software engineering, knowledge-based systems, and man-machine interfaces. The EEC, seriously concerned that its information technology industries could be given the coup de grace by Japan, has organized its own program, ESPRIT, with committed funding of 11.5 million ECU and planned funding of up to 1.5 billion ECU over five years. In 1985, plans were initiated toward a Canadian Fifth Generation Research Plan (Ref. 1).

This chapter discusses the potential impact of Fifth Generation computer technology.

Fifth Generation Technologies (Ref. 1)

Fifth Generation computing has become feasible at this point in history because of the maturity of four key research areas: artificial intelligence (including topics such as natural language interfaces and knowledge engineering), computer systems and languages, microelectronics and computer architecture. The key task of creating Fifth Generation machines is the integration of achievements and techniques from these areas.

One of the major advantages of Fifth Generation systems lies in their user interfaces. For example, natural language front ends will make it possible for untrained users to deal with computers in English, French, or Japanese. (Rudimentary natural language front ends are already commercially available.) Together with further advances in speech recognition and synthesis they will make it possible to converse with a machine as though it was a human administrative assistant. The increased use of computer graphics will further improve the man-machine interface (the Apple Macintosh has already given the marketplace a glimpse of the advances which can be achieved here). Finally, the development of "user-friendly" human interfaces depends substantially on our understanding of the term "user-friendly". Research in cognitive science will give us a better understanding of the principles underlying "user-friendly" interfaces.

Turning to another type of interface between systems and their environments, computer vision has made striking advances in recent years. It will provide machines with the ability to "see" their environments and, more importantly, to "understand" what they are seeing. This capability will be essential for robots and will also allow machine interpretation of medical films to aid physicians with diagnoses.

Perhaps the most dramatic of the developments leading us to the Fifth Generation are in knowledge engineering, the set of languages, tools and techniques used to give a computer "knowledge" about a field of human expertise. The job of transferring knowledge, from the head of a human expert to the knowledge base of an expert system, has emerged as one of the most difficult aspects of building expert systems.

The knowledge-base of an expert system may contain millions of facts. Storing them in a computer, retrieving them, protecting them from error or machine failure, sharing them among many users, and distributing them to many different machines -- these are all difficult engineering problems. Progress in computer systems and languages, which includes work in software engineering, database management and programming languages, will allow us to address these problems adequately. The development of programming environments (a programming language plus all of the related software tools used by programmers to design, specify, write, test and document their work) is particularly important here.

Commercial viability depends heavily on the speed, cost and reliability of the product, and it is here that microelectronics and hardware architecture play a key role. Microelectronics, the technology of the "chip," allows us to shrink the physical size and cost of a piece of equipment, and dramatically improve its reliability at the same time. (The size and cost of electronic circuits has been dropping by a factor of ten every three years. By way of comparison, the difference in speed between a person walking and an automobile on a freeway is a single factor of ten, and the speed of a jet airliner represents another single factor of ten.) Researchers in hardware architecture are studying new ways to design and structure computers, so that many parts of a reasoning process can be carried on simultaneously. Conventional machines are capable of doing only one thing at a time.

A New Breed of Computers

The aim of the Fifth Generation projects is not to improve on exciting computer hardware, software, and architectures. The goal is to develop an entirely new generation of computers, a generation which will obsolete today's technology in future years.

> "The Fifth Generation will not be traditional computers. Instead, they'll be symbolic inference machines capable of reasoning their way swiftly through massive amounts of knowledge and data. They'll be computers that can learn, associate, make inferences, make decisions, and otherwise behave in ways usually considered the exclusive province of human reason....Fifth Generation machines will understand spoken, written, and graphical input." (Ref. 3)

What will Fifth Generation computers do? Among the ICOT goals: An optical scanner that can read both type and pictures, an automatic translating machine that can convert Japanese text into other languages, and a typewriter with a 10,000-word vocabulary that is operated by human speech rather than touch, allowing an executive to produce a written copy of his thoughts by talking directly into a desk-top unit. The fifth generation machine may be able to perform up to 70 times more calculations each second, and have 3,000 times the internal memory of supercomputers now in use, such as the Cray-1. (Refs. 4 and 5).

The Fifth Generation computer will use advanced forms of very-large-scale-integration (VLSI) chips -- semiconductor chips that have higher component densities and are capable of much higher speeds than those available today. The Japanese machine will have new forms of computer architecture: instead of one central processor -- the "brain" of the computer -- or even several processors working simultaneously in parallel, Japan's machine might
have a million or more small processors operating in parallel. (Ref. 4)

Two target applications are language translation and consultation systems. The goal with translations is for multiple languages, a 100,000-word vocabulary, and 90% translation accuracy. The remaining 10% would be handled by humans. Consultation systems include medical diagnosis, natural-language and speech interfaces, intelligent-computer-aided design, the ability to be tailored for use as an expert consultant in diverse subjects, and computer troubleshooting and diagnosis. The goal is to include a capability for semiautomated knowledge acquisition. The computer may, for instance, monitor news reports, read books and newspapers, draw information from other computer databases, or simply listen to an academic lecture. It would decide what to remember and what to ignore with a minimal amount of human intervention. (Ref. 4)

A Major Shift in World Economics

Edward A. Feigenbaum and Pamela McCorduck in their book, *The Fifth Generation* suggest that *knowledge* will be the new wealth of nations (Ref. 6).

Specifically, how will the control of knowledge translate into dollars? First, we must recognize that the industrialized world is being transformed into an information society (Ref. 7). While about 17% of the workforce worked with information in 1985, now about 65% of workers are in information related jobs. The amount of information which any business executive must deal with is overwhelming. The computer is obviously the backbone of our new information-based society. The Japanese have targeted dominance of the computer industry with their Fifth Generation project.

Despite years of flogging exports, Japanese companies can claim merely 2% of the computer business outside Japan. They have not developed systems demonstrably more useful than those the competition offers. In most cases, they have played catch-up, refining and developing basic work in the West (Ref. 8). According to Morley and Taylor (Ref. 9), Japan discovered that about a trillion dollars had already been invested worldwide in software for IBM computers. And, that's an investment that not even the Japanese government wanted to tackle. The alternative? Obsolete that investment by changing the rules of the game and developing a new technology. Thus was created the government/industry coalition and the Fifth Generation Computer Project (Ref. 10).

Project Problems and Challenges

The pragmatics of organization, funding, and management of the advanced generation computing projects have raised some serious questions relating to problem areas which may ultimately influence their success. This section discusses some of the specific potential problems which have been identified within various projects.

First, there are potential financial problems. It was long believed that the Japanese Government is finding the project too expensive for one country alone and would like to share the financing and some of the research with at least one other country. The Japanese publication, Nikkan kogyo shimbun of 12 November 1984 reported that ICOT and the Alvey Directorate will collaborate on developing a high-level Japanese-English machine translation system using the know-how derived from Japanese and British Fifth Generation projects (Ref. 11).

A second potential problem area is project management. Most of the Fifth Generation projects have cooperative industrial sponsors. The sponsors are, in many cases, competitors. These competitive forces present the challenge of achieving real cooperative participation in research and equal sharing of results. Several of the projects have governmental sponsorship. These projects must overcome the bureaucracy that plagues many governmental programs.

However, the most important potential problem is technological. Parallel processing is likely not to be the panacea that some are predicting. Potential problems with parallel architectures are discussed in Chapter 6 of this report.

William F. Zachmann, vice president, International Data Corp. (Framingham, MA) sees serious problems in the Fifth Generation Project stemming from the flawed key assumptions underlying the basis for the entire project (Ref. 10). Zachmann identifies four key assumptions in the ICOT project: (1) Nonnumeric processing is the key to the future; (2) Current systems are inadequate for such processing; (3) New hardware architectures are required; and (4) AI and knowledge-based systems will typically be large and complex.

Zachmann suggests that these assumptions are, for the most part, wrong. He points out that: (1) Nonnumeric data has been a major part of the use of computers since the late 1950s, and that toady nearly every vendor with a serious product offering in office automation provides at least some capability to handle data, text, voice, image, and graphics; (2) All existing applied artificial intelligence and knowledge-based expert systems run perfectly well on traditional systems; and (3) While some applications will involve massive inference operations requiring brute force hardware solutions, they will by no means be typical or characteristic of the application of artificial intelligence techniques.

Summary

The goals of the Fifth Generation projects are far-reaching. The potential impact, control of a major sector of the worldwide commerce translates to a potential economic revolution.

In any research program, specific results are not known until they are discovered. While all of the initial goals of the Fifth Generation projects may not be achieved as envisioned at the time the projects were formed, it must be recognized that new and unforseen discoveries will be made along the way. It is inconceivable that multibillion dollar funding of programs employing some of the best research talent in the world will not have significant impact and greatly influence commercial technology in the next decade.

References

1. Manning, E., Cerone, N., Hold, R., Mylopoulos, J. and Voucher, J., Towards a Canadian 5th Generation Research Plan, Supplement to the Canadian Artificial Intelligence Newsletter, March 1985.

2. Hinden, Harvey, J., "Fifth-Generation Computing: Dedicated Software Is The Key," Computer Design, September 1984, pp. 150-164.

3. McCorduck, Pamela, CACM, Vol. 26, 1983, pp. 629-630.

4. Scheftner, Jim, "Fifth Generation Computers," Popular Science, April 1983, pp. 79-81.

5. Wellborn, Stanley N., "U.S., Japan Square Off Over Supercomputers," U.S. News and World Report, 5 December 1983, p. 62.

6. Feigenbaum, Edward A. and McCorduck, Pamela, The Fifth Generation, Addison-Wesley, 1983.

7. Naisbitt, John, Megatrends, Warner Books, 1984.

8. Uttal, Bro, "Here Comes Computer, Inc.," Fortune, 4 October 1982, pp. 82-90.

9. Morley, Richard E. and Taylor, William, A., Demystifiying Artificial Intelligence, Graeme Publishing Company, 1984.

10. Bergstrom, Robin P., "Here They Come Again...Maybe," Manufacturing Engineering, April 1985, pp. 69-71.

11. Robinson, Louis G., ed., "Alvey & ICOT," The Artificial Intelligence Report, December 1984, pp. 14-15.

4

A Dramatic Change in Research and Development in the United States

The commercial and industrial sectors of American business have always relied heavily on public domain and joint venture research and development projects. While in-house R&D can provide individual companies with a slight competitive edge in specialized fields, it must be recognized that cooperative R&D programs have had a greater impact on advanced technological advancements in the United States during the past two decades. The majority technologies upon which today's society is based have evolved from public domain R&D projects: the computer, the transistor, the laser, space-age materials, advanced robotics, and artificial intelligence. The past three years have seen virtually every established source of public domain R&D closed and a new spectrum of cooperative ventures arise to shape the present and future trends in R&D both in the United States and worldwide. The contemporary picture in R&D follows this scenario:

a. Worldwide competition has grown to become a greater force affecting the success of American businesses than competition within our own country. The Japanese automobile industry and Middle East petroleum industry demonstrated the power of global industrialization by thrusting the entire economy of the United States into a recession.

b. The computer has become the backbone of our society. Our businesses and governments are directed by computers and the manufacturing environment is becoming computer-integrated. Most people use computers in their jobs, ranging from engineering design to word processing, and the computer is now beginning to assume an important role in the home. Those who possess the most advanced computer technologies can translate this technology into worldwide economic power.

c. The funding associated with the research and development projects aimed toward achieving fundamental advances in computer technology is clearly beyond the capacity of any single company. Thus, national interests have arose for cooperative and government-sponsored R&D efforts for various aspects of computer technology.

d. In late 1981, after three years of planning, Japan's Ministry of International Trade and Industry (MITI) announced the Fifth Generation Computer project. Funds were committed in advance for the first three years of work. MITI pooled resources with eight of Japan's largest electronics firms to open the Institute for New Generation Computer Technology (ICOT) in April 1982. ICOT's mandate is to develop a new computer family with the software and hardware for artificial intelligence.

The aim of the project was clearly to surpass the United States in computer technology.

e. A strong response to the Japanese Fifth Generation project was generated in the United States and Europe. Antitrust policies in the U.S. were altered to allow research consortiums and research & development limited partnerships. Four major cooperatives were formed with research objectives similar to the ICOT project:

- Microelectronics & Computer Technology Corporation (MCC), Austin, Texas, USA
- Semiconductor Research Corporation (SRC), Research Triangle Park, North Carolina, USA
- European Strategic Program on Research in Information Technology (ESPRIT), Brussels, Belgium
- Alvey Program for Advanced Information Technology, London, England

These research and development consortiums have replaced the defunct avenues of public domain R&D which dominated technological advancements in the computer field previous years:

- The U.S. Department of Defense fostered the development of the field of artificial intelligence with strong sponsorship of university programs. This interest in free-spirited AI research has been superseded by the DARPA Strategic Computing Program with specific goal-directed objectives.
- The National Science Foundation's Program in Productive Research and Technology provided the development of technology in the areas of machine vision, robotics, computer-aided design, composite material processing, PCB inspection, laser measurement, and other areas. This major manufacturing-related research through universities is no longer in effect.
- The fundamental research and development programs associated with the early states of NASA's space program have been superceded by an emphasis on space commercialization by the private sector.
- The breakup of AT&T transformed Bell Laboratory from the world's largest privately operated public-domain into an in-house lab. While the developments from Bell Labs could be licensed by any American company in the past, all R&D developments will now be for proprietary commercialization within the AT&T corporation.

The research results which these programs contributed toward the United States position as the world technology leader must be replaced by other programs. Research cooperatives will play a major role in filling this gap.

5

Future Computer Hardware

Future generations of computers will be of three basic types:

1. Coventional microcomputers, minicomputers, and mainframes, for use in the home, office and factory.

2. The artificial intelligence-based computer, for processing logic inferences and emulating human behavior.

3. The supercomputer, for high-speed number crunching and massive calculations.

The development of each of these families of computers will depend upon continued improvements of the silicon chip.

The Silicon Chip

Since the invention of the integrated circuit (IC), a complete electronic circuit on a single piece of semiconductor, in 1958 by Jack Kilby at Texas Instruments, the emphasis in microprocessor design has been to put more and more components onto smaller and smaller chips. Using very large scale integration (VLSI) techniques, the number of components on semiconductor chips has approximately doubled annually since 1958.

Currently, the standard microprocessor chip is the 64K memory chip, with 65,536 bits of dynamic random access memory (RAM).

In 1982, the 32-bit microprocessor superchip was commercially introduced in the United States. The 32-bit chips by Motorola (MC 68020) and Intel (i APX 432) use CMOS technology. Other 32-bit chips using NMOS and PMOS technologies are manufactured by Bell Laboratories (Bellmac 32A), National (NS32032) and Hewlett-Packard. These chips contain between 100,000 and 450,000 transistors on a single chip.

The next step beyond 64K in chip memory is the 256K RAM chip invented at Bell Laboratories and first introduced commercially in 1983 by Western Electric. Several other chipmakers, including Motorola and Mostek in the United States, and Japan's Fujitsu and Nippon Electric will also be manufacturing 256K chips by 1988.

Researchers are continuing efforts to develop higher capacity superchips. In September 1983, IBM announced the development of an experimental 512K dynamic RAM chip. This commercialization will mark another breakthrough in computing. While state-of-the-art mainframe systems execute 4-23 mips (million instructions per second), the 512K chip is projected to execute 12 to 70 mips.

One-megabit chips are expected to appear on the market in volume in 1986. Eight companies with working prototypes, including AT&T, IBM, Hitachi, Fujitsu, and NEC, described their RAM circuits at the February 1985 International Solid State Circuits Conference.

Future Hardware (Ref. 1)

Advances in materials technology and design methodology will ultimately dicate the future of computer hardware. As very large scale integration of silicon proceeds to its physical limits, three major issues have arisen: how system designers can efficiently use such density; how circuit density can be increased even further; and how to obtain ever higher switching speeds. The call for efficient system design involves a discussion of advanced design tools such as silicon compilers.

Advanced design methods will be needed for engineers to use increasing circuit density effectively. Gate arrays and standard cells will serve the lower complexity end of the application-specific IC market. Design tools are already available for that purpose. Full custom designs, however, are a different matter. These will require the development of sophisticated silicon compilers to enable system designers to develop merchant market quality custom ICs. Such advanced design tools are emerging on the market. The next few years should see an explosive growth in silicon compilation methods to help designers cope with the increases in circuit complexity.

The search for ever greater density leads to a consideration of CMOS, its ultimate limits, and beyond that, the infant science of molecular level electronics. The quest for faster switching speed demands an examination of the present rapid progress in gallium arsenide digital circuits.

Beyond the Silicon Chip (Ref. 2)

The limits to further miniaturization of silicon chip electronics technology may be in sight. Decreasing the size of components of integrated electronic circuits even further may depend upon a rapidly emerging new technology -- molecular electronics. A typical conventional silicon chip used in an electronic watch, a pocket calculator, or a personal computer may measure 1 cm^3 and carry up to 64,000 bits of information. Size of individual elements on these chips has been reduced to 0.002 mm. But the technology used to produce today's chips may not be suitable for producing much smaller elements, on the scale of individual molecules.

Two broad, overlapping approaches dominate current thinking on how molecular-scale electronic devices might be built. One approach would depend upon synthetic materials, such as conducting polymers or charge transfer salts. The other approach would use biological polymers, primarily proteins. These could serve to make frameworks to which molecular-scale conductors and functional components could be attached. It might even be possible to genetically engineer microorganisms to produce complete integrated circuits. However they are made, molecular-scale integrated circuits will be much more compact than existing chips and available at a much lower cost per element.

Gallium Arsenide Chips (Ref. 3)

Recent progress in gallium arsenide IC development has produced some surprising results. Once thought of as a very high speed, but low yield, power hungry technology most suitable for discrete transistor and SSI applications, GaAs ICs can now achieve both LSI complexity and low-power dissipation. Laboratories in the United States, Japan, and Europe are demonstrating GaAs LSI chips that have substantially better speed and power parameters. Although current GaAs results are experimental, laboratory development devices, the amount of research going on lends credibility to recent technology forecasts for significant use of GaAs in high-speed digital logic systems before the end of the decade.

Supercomputers

Supercomputers are special application machines used for data intensive tasks such as weather simulation, airplane modeling, bomb trajectory, earthquake prediction, military strategies, and the production of animation in movies. The Cray-1 can theoretically run at 140 megaflops (million operations per second), and the Cyber 205, it's claimed, can perform 800 megaflops for rare categories of pure mathematical calculations. But in practice, programming complexities often limit both machines to 20 megaflops. Mainframes, for comparison, are typically rated at around 2 megaflops. Costing between $5 million and $15 million, there are only 60 to 100 supercomputers now in service, primarily used by governments, especially in defense laboratories.

The Cray-1 supercomputer contains 250,000 memory and logic chips, wired together with 70 miles of cable. The 5-ton machine is packed so densely that its microworld of components can not drain off the heat produced. The circuits must be chilled by a lattice containing liquid coolant. Without this refrigeration, the Cray-1 would actually melt through the floor in a few minutes. Computing speeds are on the order of 400 million calculations per second for short bursts.

Under current development is the Cray-2, which will use 256K chips to double the speed of the Cray-1. Control Data Corporation is endeavoring to develop a 10 gigaflop (10 billion calculations per second) supercomputer for delivery by the end of 1986.

Computer for AI

In the early days of artificial intelligence research, most programming was done on big computers, such as the DEC-KL-10, with memory-intensive compilers for the AI languages such as LISP. In the mid-1970s, researchers at MIT developed a design for a dedicated machine to process LISP directly. This technology was licensed to two firms in 1980, and "LISP Machines" or personal AI computers have been available for several years.

It now appears that LISP dialects designed specifically for personal computers will become commonplace. It is also expected that software portability will improve substantially. PROLOG and its derivatives, now prevalent throughout Europe, will become incorporated with LISP in the United States. It is expected that the price of good AI personal computers that run LISP will continue to drop as competition heats up and demand escalates.

Parallel architectures are now being considered for future AI machines. This is especially attractive for PROLOG because its structure facilitates parallel search. Japan intends to build a sequential PROLOG personal computer 1985, featuring 10K logical inferences per second. In the 1990 time frame, Japan's Fifth Generation Computer Project is projected to yield a enormously powerful AI parallel processing machine running PROLOG at one billion logical inferences per second (about 10,000 times more powerful than the DEC-KL-10 with which the AI community grew up).

Personal Computers (Ref 5)

Michael Dertouzos, director of MIT's computer science laboratory, sees personal computer technology maturing in three stages. The stages are based on successive generations of operating systems -- the housekeeping programs that manage a computer's internal operations and that also contain software tools for writing, debugging, and transferring programs. The first generation of personal computers, which Dertouzos sees as nearing its end, uses operating systems such as CP/M and MS-DOS, designed for machines with limited memory and disk-storage capacity. He sees the second generation, now emerging, as based largely on Unix and Unix derivatives. Dertouzos predicts that before this decade is out, Unix machines will be supplanted by advanced, highly integrated personal computers similar to today's LISP machines. In these machines, the present sharp distinction between operating systems and programming languages will be blurred -- in effect, the language will be part of the operating system itself. Easy to operate, programmed to obey commands phrased in rudimentary English or other human languages able to create and display dazzlingly detailed color images, these machines will be exquisitely easy to use.

References

1. Bond, J., "Future Hardware," Computer Design, September 1984, pg. 209.

2. Molecular Electronics: Beyond the Silicon Chip, Technical Insights, 1983.

3. Reeder, T. M., "High Speed Systems Look To GaAs For Low Power LSI," Computer Design, September 1984, pp 231-246.

4. Bond, J., "Circuit Density and Speed Boost Tomorrow's Hardware," Computer Design, September 1984, pp 210-225.

5. Alexander, Tom, "The Next Revolution In Computer Programming," Fortune, October 29, 1984, pp 81-86.

6

Future Computer Architectures

Japan's Fifth Generation Computer Project has aimed the primary focus of its research at incorporating parallel processing in its new breed of computers. This emphasis and the potential impact of a new breed of computers has caused parallel processing to be a topic of great current public interest and controversey.

Architecture refers to the general design of a computer's circuitry, the overall logical scheme by which it takes in information, manipulates it, and produces results. Current computers use a so-called von-Neumann architecture, where a single central processing unit performs each step of a calculation serially, one after another. When large amounts of data must be processed, this one-step-at-a-time processing is too slow. Parallel processing techniques provide an alternative compute which can allow large problems to be solved faster, based on the premise that dividing a problem into smaller parts will yield faster results. The underlying concept behind all new parallel architectures is to have small blocks of tightly coupled processor memory elements divide the algorithm and parallel process its parts concurrently. As a result, larger problems can be solved faster.

Scientific and engineering problems of the next decade will require an increase in speed of at least two orders of magnitude over the fastest current machines such as the Cray-2. Most experts agree that some form of parallel processing must be implemented to meet these demands.

The application requirements of a computer determine the most appropriate type of architecture. Von Neumann architectures are appropriate for data processing tasks with procedural languages. Supercomputers, designed for solving large scale numerical calculations in engineering and science, utilize single assignment languages. Fifth Generation computers, on the other hand, are aimed at knowledge-based systems applications operating with predicate logic languages. Thus, there are three candidates for future architectures -- thoe that are either control driven (von Neumann systems), data driven (super computers), or demand driven (fifth generation systems). The distinctions between the knowledge-intensive and supercomputer areas, however, are not clear. There are already efforts to incorporate parallel processing into supercomputers. The Cray X-MP and Cray-2, for example, will have two to four processors.

The potential design of machines with a million processors operating in parallel would intuitatively appear to make possible an improvement in processing speeds by a factor of a million, resulting in revolutionary improvements in the performance of intelligent software. However, miraclesmay take a little longer. AI authority Dr. Douglas Lenat found that when he had the expert system EURISKO simulate the action of a progressively increasing number of parallel processors working simultaneously on tasks from its agenda, he found that once four processors had been simulated, the rate at which the program made significant discoveries did not increase further. The reason for this was that in completing its top ranked task, EURISKO usually discovered a new task it found more interesting than the rest of its original agenda. Where good heuristics allow such a "best-first" search, parallel processing may have diminishing returns (Ref. 1).

The key issue in parallel processing a single application is the resultant processing speedup achieved, depending on the number of processors used. Forthcoming research must show which problems are "parallelizable." It is likely that certain tasks, such as model-based vision system processing and speech understanding may benefit greatly from parallel processing. Other knowledge intensive areas may benefit less dramatically from parallel processing techniques. One should remember that most hard problems have search trees that grow exponentially. Even a millionfold increase in computing power will not change the fact that most problems can only be solved through the judicious application of knowledge to limit the search, and not by brute force.

References

1. Lenat, Douglas B., "Computer Software for Intelligent Systems," Scientific American, Vol. 251, No. 3, September 1984, pp. 204-213.

2. Mokhoff, Nicolas, "Future Architecture," Computer Design, September 1984, p. 103.

3. Mokhoff, Nicolas, "Parallelism Makes Strong Bid for Next Generation Computers," Computer Design, September 1984, pp. 104-131.

4. Schefter, Jim, "Fifth-Generation Computer, Popular Science, April 1983, pp. 79+.

7

Future Computer Software

The software industry in the United States, expected to reach $40 billion in sales by 1986, suffers from insufficient reliability and poor maintainability of software products, frequent overruns in development costs, and high rates of personnel turnover. Future software engineering will attempt to overcome these problems with automated tools designed to reduce costs, increase reliability, and build better programs in a structured manner. A major trend will be software for artificial intelligence-based machines, supercomputers, and personal computers which are dedicated to individual applications.

Problems In Software Development (Ref. 1)

The costs of computing can be conveniently divided into hardware and software costs. It is useful to see how the proportion between them has shifted. In the early days of computing, costs were generally considered to be about 20% software and 80% hardware. In 1982, Graham reported that hardware costs were about 30% of the total, leaving 70% to software (Ref. 2). Others have suggested that hardware costs may be as low as 20%. One can easily argue the specifics, but the trend is clear, computing costs are being driven by software, not hardware. As hardware costs continue to decline and personnel costs rise, the elementary economics of substitution tell us to replace labor with hardware, i.e., to automate. The management implications are significant. At the 20% hardware-cost level, a doubling of hardware costs can be fully offset by a 25% software cost reduction.

It is interesting to speculate about the reasons for these high software costs. Most would agree that the process of software development, to which we will return, is a mixture of art and science, although it might be difficult to find consensus on the split. If the process were producing proper, timely results, there would be little concern that it is not pure science. Unfortunately, the results have often been poor. The scientific aspects have been subjected to analysis and improvement, but the artistic elements have so far eluded progress. A 1979 General Accounting Office Report on software development contracts (Ref. 3) found that 50% went over cost, 60% went over schedule, and only 2% of the software was usable as delivered.

Future Software (Ref. 4)

Because software has such an inherently long development cycle, the software under development today will probably not be operational until the 1990s. But, with software designs for operating systems, languages, and applications inseparable from future computer architectures and hardware, the situation becomes more complicated. For example, parallel architectures require languages with parallel control structures. Chips that implement parallel software algorithms need architectures such as data flow designs geared to concurrency.

The software currently under development for the 1990s is characterized by a lack of standards, and by honest differences of opinion as to which is "best." Perhaps the best example of these is the "conflict" between so-called flavors of the LISP and PROLOG AI languages. Such problems pertain for lesser known software as well. It is just too early to say which are the best solutions to the many problems of the software design community. Major efforts are under way in Japan, the United States, England, and Europe to address these problems. Similar work is going on in Canada, Australia, and other countries.

Japan's Development of Software Technology (Ref. 5)

Currently, Japan is trying to extend its successful experience in technology buildup via national R&D projects to the software area. The intent of the Fifth-Generation Computer System Project, in particular, is to push Japan to the forefront of computer system technology by 1990. The government plans to pour $45 million into the Fifth Generation project during the first three years, 1982-84, and total project cost might reach several billion dollars. The project involves R&D talent from government agencies, industries, and universities and deals with several key technologies, including software engineering.

The Evolution of Software Engineering (Ref. 6)

Progress in software engineering -- the science of producing economical, reliable software -- will occur over the rest of this decade, as software development evolves from an art into a science. Of all the efforts contributing to software engineering, standardization, specification, and testing are the weakest. Standardization is slowly occuring, driven by the need to make software portable and reusable (to overcome escalating development costs and manpower shortages). However, much must be done with specifications and testing before software engineering is a reality.

In order to develop software, requirements must be specified, architectural features must be defined, functions must be specified, and programming, testing, and integration must be done. The software development process requires repeated iteration of these tasks until system tests are successfully completed.

Various software architectural concepts are emerging for developing portable, reusable, and maintainable software. These include the virtual machine (to protect software from hardware changes) and information hiding through layering of software functions. Layering protects high-level software functions from changes in low-level software implementations.

Another concept provides functional independence between major software elements through formalized interfaces, allowing software design teams to set up and test system functions easily and independently. Software designers may also allow for function migration between processors through module interface standardization, common operating system functions, and loose coupling between modules. With formalized and flexible interfaces, modularity and loose coupling allow system growth from a single processor to a multiprocessor configuration with minimal software changes.

These ideas lead to the software bus concept (a standard interface for software run time and development environments). Such buses will first occur for a specific manufacturer's products. True standardization (among all manufacturers) will occur much later, if at all. It is usually not in the economic interest of manufacturers (especially chipmakers) to make software portable to outside machines.

Once standard interfaces are defined, different organizations can develop software packages that will work together via a common standardized operating system. Thus, operating system and software bus standardization will lead to the creation of portable and reusable software plug-in modules.

Function distribution is yet another architectural trend that will grow in this decade. Function distribution occurs because of VLSI's dramatic hardware cost reductions. For example, the increasing availability of cheaper and more powerful microprocessors allows the implementation of distributed computer system architectures.

Distributed architecture, in turn, affects software architecture. For example, software becomes modularized into "functions," and functional packages become distributed in various processors. Thus, because a processor may not contain all functions within itself, it requests other network processors to provide the needed services. Interface and message protocol standardization is necessary to control and to manage the complexity introduced by function distribution.

Dedicated Software (Ref. 7)

In the future, three distinct, but overlapping computer types will dominate -- the artificial intelligence-based machine that simulates human behavior; the supercomputer geared to high speed number crunching and massive calculations; and the "standard" home, factory, or office machine, be it micro, mini, or mainframe. With fine-tuned software, the AI computer will use languages that optimize its symbolic processing and logic manipulations.

Meanwhile, the supercomputer will use software geared to its highly parallel architecture, and the "run-of-the-mill" machine will feature easy-to-use, portable software that facilitates the networked home, office, and factory.

The Fifth Generation should blossom by the beginning of the 1990s, and consist of symbolic processing with extensive AI applications. Moreover, software geared to parallel processing and supercomputers may sport concurrent processing languages and functional programming. Older software cannot do the job with parallel processing-based architectures because it is based, to a large extent, on the classic procedure-data computation machine/software model. Software for this von Neumann model is said to be program control statement driven. In other words, program instructions execute only when the program's control statements give the order. Such software draws a distinction between manipulated data and the procedures that perform the manipulation. Other software types, especially more recently developed languages, make no such distinction. Parallel architecture design is a young, still-evolving field with no clearly discernible trends. Unresolved issues include how the parallel processes communicate to result in a combination of parallel computations for the program's "answers," and the number of processors that should be in parallel as well as their size, memory, and design. There are also questions of cost, the need for specialized programming languages unknown to the computing community at large, the need for specialized algorithms for parallel computation, the unknown quality of the VLSI that will be available (i.e., speed and packaging), the theoretical advantages of the parallel architecture under consideration, and more.

Artificial Intelligence Software

There are three general families of languages used for artificial intelligence programming: (1) functional applications languages such as LISP, (2) logic programming languages such as PROLOG, and (3) object-oriented languages such as SMALLTALK and ACTOR.

Many AI programs are written in LISP (LIST Processing), which was developed by John McCarthy at MIT in the early 1960s. LISP is an easy programming language to learn, primarily because it has a simple syntax. LISP programs and data are both in the same form-lists. Thus, AI programs can manipulate other AI programs. This allows programs to create or modify other programs, an important feature in intelligent applications. It also allows programming aids for debugging and editing to be written in LISP, providing great interactive flexibility for the LISP programmer, who can thus tailor things to suit his needs.

PROLOG is a theorem-proving, logic-oriented language developed in 1973 at the University of Marseille AI Laboratory by A. Colmerauer and P. Roussel. Additional work on PROLOG has been done at the University of Edinburgh in Great Britain. Development of PROLOG in France has continued achieving a documented system that can be run on nearly all computers. PROLOG has proved very popular in Europe and is now targeted as the language of Japan's Fifth Generation Computer Project. PROLOG's design (and its powerful pattern matcher) is well suited to parallel search and therefore an excellent candidate for such powerful future computers incorporating parallel processing. Substantial interest in PROLOG is now arising in the United States, with some of PROLOG's features being implemented in LISP.

An emerging trend is the increased use of object-oriented programming to ease the creation of large exploratory programs. The use of objects is also a good way to program dynamic symbolic simulations, which will become more important as the quest for utilizing deeper knowledge accelerates and the demand for increased reliability of knowledge-based systems is pursued. Object-oriented programming also holds promise for distributed processing, as each object could be implemented on a separate processor in a linked network of processors.

References

1. Hutchinson, G. K., and Clementson, A. T., "Manufacturing Control Systems: An Approach To Reducing Software Costs," presented at the International Conference of the Future, MIT, 9-12 October 1984

2. Graham, Alan K., "Software Design: Breaking the Bottleneck," IEEE Spectrum, March 1982.

3. General Accounting Office Report FGMSD-80-4, "Contracting for Computer Software Development," September 1979.

4. Hindin, H. J., "Future Software," Computer Design, September, 1984, pg. 149.

5. Kim, K. H., "A Look At Japan's Development of Software Engineering Technology," Computer, May 1983, pp. 26-38.

6. Batni, R. P., "Software Development Evolves Into Software Engineering," Computer Design, September 1984, pp. 165-181.

7. Hindin, H. J., "Fifth-Generation Computing: Dedicated Software Is The Key," Computer Design, September 1984, pp. 150-164.

8

Institute for New Generation Computer Technology (ICOT)

As computerization advances, information technology with computers as its core has been applied to various areas of society, and has become an indispensable tool in society.

To provide for the conditions and information demands of the 1990s, more advanced and higher-level functions and performance will be required of information technology; this includes utilization of more varied media, easy-to-use computers, higher software productivity and application of information technology to those areas in which existing information technology has not been applied.

In order to meet these needs, the design philosophy of the current computer technology should be studied and evaluated.

Conventional computers, following the von Neumann computer architecture, are now realized by the simplest hardware because when the first computers were invented, the hardware was expensive and bulky. Most of the functions required are then realized by software to provide an efficient processing system. Therefore, the conventional computers have become numerical-processing oriented and stored-program sequential processing systems. High speed and large memory capacity have been pursued from the economic standpoint, producing the present enormously big computer systems.

However, the situation has evolved as follows.

1. VLSIs have substantially reduced hardware costs, so computer systems can use as much hardware as required.
2. A new architecture for parallel processing is now required because device speed has approached the limit for sequential processing.
3. Parallel processing should be realized in order to utilize effective mass production of VLSIs.
4. The current computer technology lacks the basic functions for nonnumeric processing of speech, text, graphics and patterns, and for artificial intelligence fields such as inference, association, and learning.

From these reasons, the Fifth Generation Computer Systems (FGCS) should be developed, providing knowledge information processing systems. FGCS should thus employ latest research results in VLSI technology, as well as technology of distributed processing, software engineering, knowledge engineering, artificial intelligence, and pattern information processing.

Thus we have concluded that it is meaningful to pursue research and development of the FGCS as innovative information technology. The goals of FCGS are to conduct creative research in this field, and to contribute to the benefit of all humankind.

Research and Development Themes

The Fifth Generation Computer Systems aim at knowledge information processing based on innovative inference functions and technologies that meet the needs anticipated in the 1990s, including intelligent interaction between man and machine and inference using knowledge bases.

The functions required of such a system can be broadly divided into four types:

1. Problem-Solving and Inference Function

This function is intended to enable the system to find solutions to problems by carrying on logical reasoning using data and knowledge stored in the system as well as information given to it from outside. This capability covers deductive inference, inductive inference, including guessing based on incomplete knowledge, and cooperative problem solving by mutual complementation of several bodies of knowledge.

2. Knowledge-Base Function

This function is aimed at providing systematic storage and retrieval of not only so-called data but also reasonable judgements and test results organized into a knowledge. Besides knowledge accumulation, it includes knowledge representation tailored to problem solving, knowledge acquisition and updating, and simultaneous utilization of distributed knowledge sources.

3. Intelligent-Interface Function

This function is intended to enable computers to handle speech, graphics, and images so that computers can interact with humans flexibly and smoothly. It might be regarded as giving computers the equivalents of human eyes, mouth, and ears, but its primary objective is to provide computers with a linguistic ability close to that of humans.

4. Intelligent-Programming Function

This function is intended to enhance the intelligence of computers so that they can take over the burden of programming from humans. While its ultimate goal is to achieve an ability to automatically convert problems into efficient computer programs, the function is aimed primarily at achieving a modular programming system and program verification system and at establishing a specification description language.

To achieve these four functions requires the development of innovative technologies encompassing the diverse fields of architecture, hardware, and software. The major research and development themes are listed below.

a. Architecture, hardware, and software to achieve the inference function. This will include:
   1. An inference mechanism based on a distributed control-based architecture that is oriented to parallel processing instead of sequential processing.
   2. Basic software to manage and execute parallel inference.

b. Hardware, architecture, and software to achieve the knowledge-base function. This will include:
   1. A knowledge-base mechanism based on structured memory instead of one-dimensional memory.
   2. Basic software to manage knowledge-bases for high-speed retrieval and relational storage of knowledge data.

c. Hardware architecture and software to achieve the intelligent interface function. This will include:
   1. An intelligent interface mechanism composed of a voice or a signal processor and other devices.
   2. Basic software for natural language processing and graphics and image understanding to ensure flexible human-machine interaction.

d. Software to achieve intelligent programming. This will include:
   1. Basic software for automatic creation of optimum programs.

New Application Fields

The knowledge information processing systems realized by the Fifth Generation Computers are expected to extensively expand the fields where computers are applied, such as manufacturing, service, engineering, and office and business management.

VLSI CAD, machine translation, and consultation systems are chosen to develop as the model systems to apply the basic Fifth Generation software, as well as to prove and assess the basic software system. The development of these application systems is planned in the intermediate and later stages.

Research and Development Plans

The research and development goals of the Fifth Generation Computer Systems are such core functions for the knowledge information processing as problemsolving, inference systems, and knowledge-base systems, that cannot be handled within the framework of conventional computer systems.

FGCS is expected to move toward the target systems through a lengthy process of trial and error, producing many original ideas along the way.

In Japan, little effort has been made in research on the key technologies, particularly software and basic theories. The research in this field should be promoted because it has a great influence on the development of hardware technology, including computer architectures and VLSIs.

Since this project aims at computer technology for the 1990s, the plans encompass wide extensions of basic technology. The FGCS project is planned to span over a period of 10 years, divided, as shown in Figure 1, into three stages: the initial stage, the intermediate stage, and the final stage.

The emphasis in the research and development of the initial stage is on accumulating the research achievements of the past in the field of knowledge information processing, and evaluating and restructuring them. In addition, candidates for each research subject have to be screened and basic technology is developed for the intermediate stage.

The research and development of the intermediate stage is focused on establishing computation models as the basis for software and hardware as well as algorithms and basic architecture based on the evaluations of the initial stage. Small- to medium-scale subsystems are then built.

The final stage puts an emphasis on the appropriate functions of both software and hardware systems, interfacing to maximize these functions, and the architecture for the total system.

Concerning the overall flow of research and development efforts, the initial stage is envisioned that software and hardware modules, and some experimental systems configured by integrating these modules, are built. These systems include hardware and software simulators, prototypes for language processing, and experimental natural language processing systems.

The intermediate stage is mainly devoted to improving and extending the results of the initial stage, and integrating them into inference and knowledge-base subsystems.

In the early part of the final stage, the configurations of these software and hardware systems developed in the intermediate stage are viewed and evaluated. The total system is developed, integrating the subsystems in order to define the ultimate goals clearly.

Table 1 describes each research item planned in the initial stage. Figure 2 is the overview of the research and development in the initial stage which shows the relationships among each research item.

Research in the initial stage of the Fifth Generation Computer Systems Project is based on the new programming language, the Version 0 Kernel Language, which is extended on Prolog. The

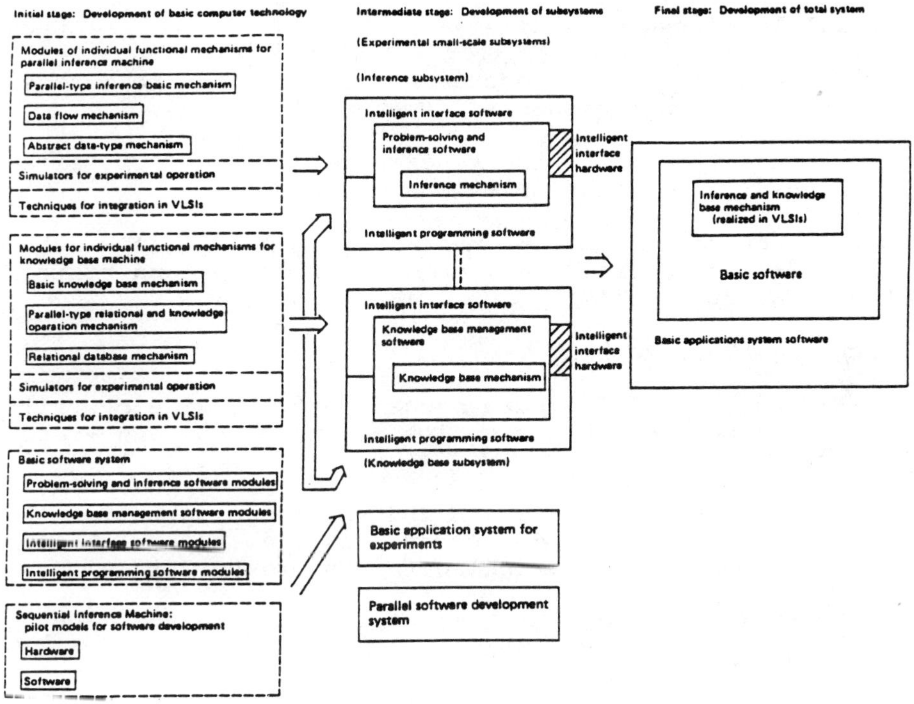

Figure 1. Stages of Fifth Generation computer research & development in the Japanese ICOT project. (source: Institute for New Generation Computer Technology)

TABLE I

Research and Development Themes in the Initial Stage of the ICOT Fifth Generation Project

A. Parallel Inference Machine

1. A parallel-type inference basic mechanism to manage the parallel execution of inference operations.

2. A data flow mechanism to execute inference operations and rapidly determine solutions.

3. An abstract data-type mechanism to consolidate detailed inference operations into several groups and control them by group.

B. Knowledge Base Machine

1. A basic knowledge-base mechanism to provide overall management of the execution of basic knowledge-base operations.

2. A parallel-type relation and knowledge operation mechanism to provide speedy knowledge accumulation, retrieval and updating, data conversion, etc.

3. A relational data base mechanism to provide large-capacity knowledge accumulation, storage, and management.

C. Basic System Software

1. Problem solving and inference software module.

2. Knowledge-base management software module.

3. Intelligent interface software module.

4. Intelligent programming software module.

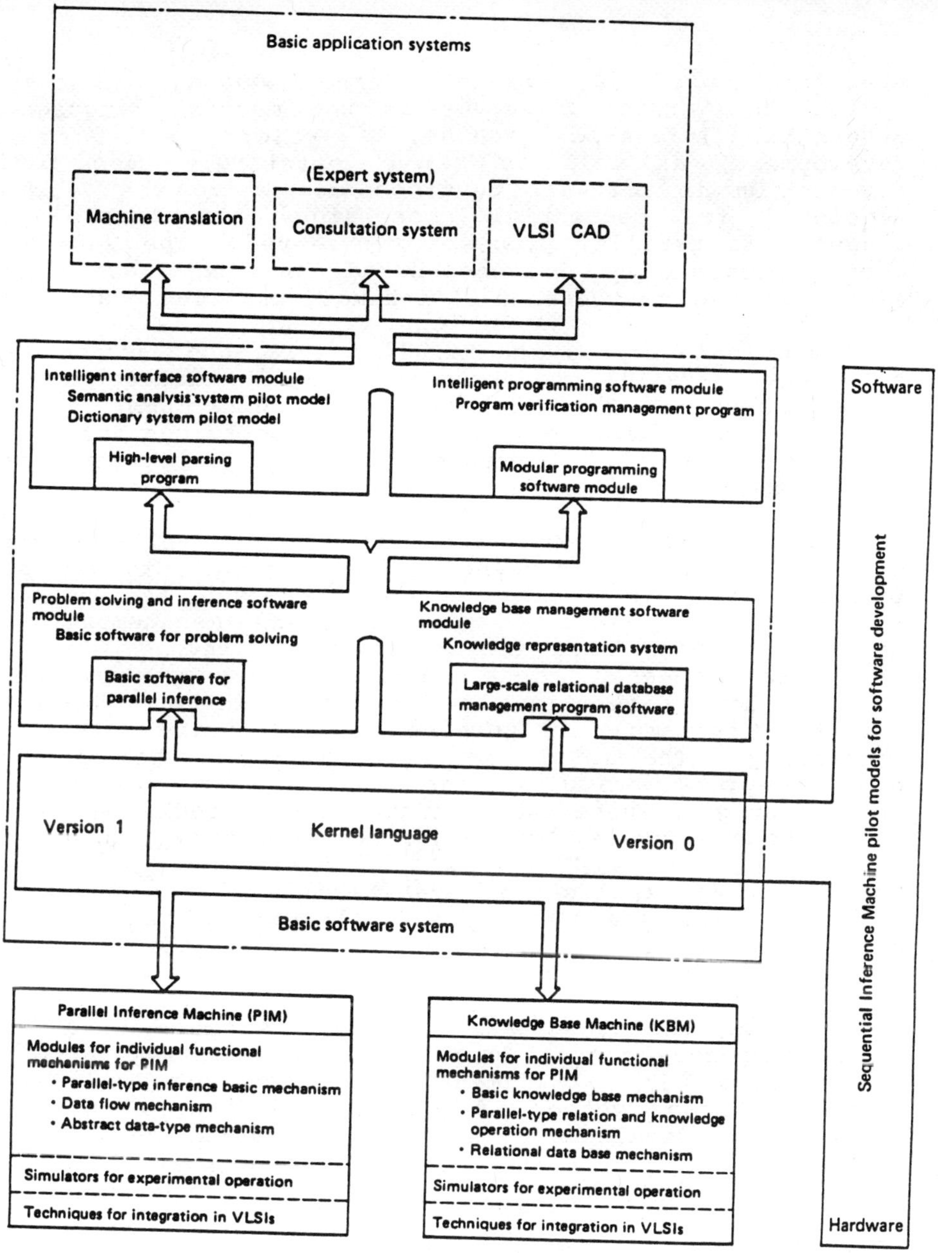

Figure 2. Overview of research and development in the initial stage of the development of the Fifth Generation Computer. (source: Institute for New Generation Computer Technology)

specification of the Version 0 Kernel Language was completed in 1982. The Version 0 serves as the machine language for the Sequential Inference Machine, a pilot model for software development, as well as being tentatively used for program description in software development. While the Version 0 was developed for sequential processing, the Version 1 Kernel Language is parallel processing oriented. The Version 1 is a logic programming language-based on the accumulation of experiences on the Version 0 with new functions added.

As shown in Figure 2, the Parallel Inference Machine (PIM) is a high-level parallel processor to directly execute the Version 1 Kernel Language. The Knowledge Base Machine (KBM) is responsible for high-speed execution of knowledge operations derived from the study on knowledge representation and relational data base operations.

The Fifth Generation software comprises two software modules: a problem solving and inference software module for the purpose of problem processing, and a knowledge-base management software module for knowledge accumulation and management. The two software modules have two hierarchical levels. On the lower level are the descriptions, or execution supporting systems, to provide various functions on the upper level. The intelligent interface systems main purpose is to realize natural language processing. The intelligent programming system for realizing automatic programming remains in a preliminary form in this initial stage. These two software modules could be also regarded as having two levels, but rather complementary than hierarchical.

The elementary application systems in the top of the figure is half-experimental and half-practical systems that are expected to develop in the intermediate stage based on the research results of the basic software systems.

Among these, the consultation system has established technology. It is purposely chosen to prove and assess the basic software system and its preliminary version called Experimental Knowledge-Based System, is planned to develop in the initial stage. This development is understood as an additional subject to Table 1.

Research issues in the ICOT Project (Ref. 2)

The FGCS project raises several research issues and directions where the ICOT project differs from some of the other advanced computing projects. These issues are:

1. Logic Programming vs. Functional Programming

At present, some researchers claim functional programming is the missing link needed to unify and connect the new computers and the new trends. In ICOT's view, however, logic programming will be the better base that unifies these different branches. Logic programming here refers to an idea utilizing in programming a type of logic such as predicate logic.

Robert Kowalski at Imperial College is one of the first advocates of logic programming. An example of programming language based on logic programming is Prolog. It was created by a group led by Alain Colmerauer of the University of L'aix Marseille. Several other groups, especially at the University of Edinburgh, have developed it further.

The commitment of Prolog and logic programming is to some, the most surprising aspect of the project and has generated a lot of questions.

It is only fair to mention that many researchers have already pointed out, locally or partly, the mutual relationships among these different branches of computer science. There is a single string tying all these branches neatly together. This string is what Kowalski calls the missing link.

2. Prolog vs. LISP

Functional programming is another candidate in the search for a unified view. LISP is the most popular functional language. (Precisely speaking, however, the LISP in common use is no longer a purely functional language.)

There are several arguments in the Prolog vs. LISP debates. One is the difference between logic programming and functional programming. Logic programming languages, Prolog, for instance, have two characteristics that functional languages such as LISP do not. The first is a function of pattern matching through unification. The second is nondeterminism. In this sense, Prolog can be considered an extension of LISP.

Some researchers insist that introducing nondeterminism is detrimental to a programming language. The FGCS view, however, is that it is not. Rather, it is a natural and useful feature of extension and is especially useful in formulating problem solving. Of course, some risk is involved, just as there is danger in, for example, "iteration" or "loop" if used in the wrong way. Thus, it may just be that some of the prejudice against nondeterminism is historically rooted.

The applications of the new computer systems envisioned include knowledge engineering. Expert systems can be defined as rule-based systems in which languages called "production" systems are widely in use. Nondeterminism is needed for production systems and rule-based systems.

Another criticism of nondeterminism is that it impedes algorithmic thinking. On the contrary, however, basic algorithmic thinking can and should be placed within the framework of logic programming. Refinement and optimization of programs are naturally carried out within this framework.

The Prolog vs. LISP debate also swirls around software accumulation. LISP has long been used in artificial intelligence research. Needless to say, the value of the software accumulation around it should be appreciated. It represents the result of considerable effort on the part of many researchers. However, a software accumulation problem still exists for the many dialects of LISP.

At some stage, greater weight should be given to new language development than to software accumulation. Consider LISP itself in comparison with FORTRAN or COBOL. The software accumulation problem is indeed a double-edged sword in terms of defending a LISP culture.

In Japan, there is another reason for choosing Prolog over LISP. Given the general lack of software accumulation in LISP in this country, from the software viewpoint, there is really little difference in the choice of languages available. This makes it both possible and advisable to discount software accumulation as a factor and opt for what is a better language on the basis of its other merits. Ironically, there is a greater freedom deviated from existing constraint.

Yet one more argument centers around LISP and Prolog. It is a point of contention that the most important thing is not the language but the programming environment.

However, this does not rule out the choice of a Prologlike language. At present, the current programming environment Prolog offers is comparatively poor; a drawback due simply to a lack of long history. Potentially Prolog has not yet demonstrated any limitation in this area and may offer greater possibilities. Thus, Prolog was chosen for this project as a basis for future research.

(3) Knowledge Engineering and the Expert Systems

Knowledge engineering is a crucial factor in the development of future computer systems. Such systems can expand the scope of computer application. Moreover, the techniques employed in knowledge engineering will be reflected in deciding what computers should be. Research on expert systems will create a new symbiosis of coexistence between human beings and computers. Therefore, this project emphasizes the necessity of unifying knowledge engineering and various computer technologies. If it succeeds in this unification, many of society's problems can be solved.

Some people question the approach to knowledge engineering taken in this project. Considerable criticism has been voiced, especially of the emphasis on logic.

In knowledge engineering, knowledge is more important than logic. In expert systems, expertise is the key. At the same time, good formalism is also important, although research on only formalism will not lead to a successful conclusion. Therefore, both logic and knowledge are essential factors, the necessary vehicles, so to speak, in developing expert systems. At the start of the project, the strategy is to establish a technical foundation based on the framework of logic.

Actually, both logic and knowledge are being pursued. Expert systems can be better built on a logic-base, or in a logic language.

(4) Artificial Intelligence and New Machines

Although artificial intelligence (AI) is already a common term, more basic research in this field is required. At the same time, study is needed on how to apply it to the real world. Actually, people are just beginning to appreciate the possibilities of AI.

To support both this basic research, as well as the application of artificial intelligence, more powerful computers are needed. Is simply the natural and gradual technical improvement of current computer technology, a conservative extension of it, all that is needed to obtain these more powerful machines? The answer must be that a conservative extension would be greatly insufficient to apply even a limited part of AI to the real world. A much greater increase in the power of computers must be achieved.

Accordingly, research on artificial intelligence will provide a base on which more powerful computers can be designed. In turn, once these more powerful machines are available, research in AI will also be enhanced.

Considerable research activity is underway in the attempt to develop more powerful tools for research into artificial intelligence. LISP machines are one such example, and should be appreciated for demonstrating the vast possibilities for future research.

In this project Prolog machines or Prologlike language machines will be developed instead.

(5) Research in Parallel Architectures

A question often asked is why hardware research is included in the FGCS project. Research in software is of course crucial. However, powerful tools, i.e., hardware, are needed to conduct software research adequately. The importance of having powerful tools explains this research on hardware.

Logic programming is expected to be a bridge connecting new software technology and new computer architecture. Present LISP and Prolog machines are a good start toward this future architecture. However, the current architecture of LISP and Prolog machines is not fundamentally different from present computer architecture.

In order to obtain the greater power needed, parallelism or ultraparallelism is required. The possibility of developing parallel computers depends on VLSI technology. The concept of logic programming is also useful in realizing this parallelism.

There are several approaches to research on parallel architecture. Plans in this project call first for research on data flow machines. This has given rise to a lot of questions as to why only data flow machines. However, there is no intention to limit research to only data flow machines. The conviction simply is that data flow machines will provide an evidence to this research in terms of parallel architecture as well as in terms of its connection with functional programming. The data flow machine is one direction worth trying.

However, the actual intention is to explore various possibilities of realizing parallel architecture, starting with data flow.

There are several approaches to research on parallel architecture other than data flow architecture. One involves reduction machines. Research on an ultraparallel machine based on the concept of production systems is reported. As mentioned before, production systems are very similar to logic programming.

It is once again emphasized that the concept of logic is the best principle on which to examine parallel architecture.

These studies on various types of parallel machines support the conjecture that such research will be undertaken more actively in the future.

This project will also attempt to explore parallelism in many ways.

References

1. Moto-oka, T., ed., "Fifth Generation Computer Systems," Proceedings of International Conference on Fifth Generation Systems, Japan Information Processing Development Center (North-Holland, 1982).

2. Kowalski, R., "Logic Programming for the Fifth Generation," Proc. Int. Conf. on Fifth Generation Systems: Dawn to the Second Computer Age (SPL Int. 1982).

9

Microelectronics and Computer Technology Corporation (MCC)

Microelectronics and Computer Technology Corporation (MCC) is a private sector joint research and development venture created to help maintain U.S. technological preeminence and international competitiveness in microelectronics and computers.

MCC began formal operations in January 1983, under the direction of retired Admiral B. R. Inman, Chairman, President and Chief Executive Officer. The need for a cooperative R&D effort by U.S. companies to develop a broad base of fundamental technologies that go significantly beyond current state-of-the-art was first proposed by William C. Norris, Chairman and Chief Executive Officer of Control Data Corporation.

MCC will concentrate scarce financial and intellectual resources that individual companies could not or would not otherwise deploy alone. It will develop technology to allow its founding and future shareholders to derive products and services of their own conception and design, and to compete in markets of their choice.

MCC's existence will also help U.S. computer and semiconductor firms meet the challenge from government-supported R&D programs that have allowed firms in Japan and Western Europe to target U.S. industries.

The following corporations currently participate in MCC as shareholders:

- Advanced Micro Devices, Inc.
- Allied Corporation
- BMC Industries, Inc.
- Boeing Corporation
- Control Data Corporation
- Digital Equipment Corporation
- Eastman Kodak Co.
- Gould, Inc.
- Harris Corporation
- Honeywell, Inc.
- Lockheed Missiles and Space Co.
- Martin Marietta Aerospace
- Mostek Corporation
- Motorola Corporation
- National Semiconductor Corp.
- NCR Corporation
- RCA Corporation
- Rockwell
- Sperry Corporation

MCC Founding

MCC was founded by William C. Norris, founder and Chairman of the Board of Control Data Corporation. He recognized that individual companies could not bring sufficient focus to bear to achieve breakthroughs, that we were not at a place in time where we'd gotten the quick return on capital in the information-handling industry, and that the R&D for the next series of gains were going to be substantially more capital-intensive.

In February 1982, he arranged a meeting of senior executives from companies in Orlando, Florida. This group agreed to do two things: to create MCC and to put together task teams to define the areas of research we would undertake. Out of those efforts came four projects and some very broad sets of goals. The shortest project concerns the packaging of integrated circuits: it lasts six years. The software technology project lasts seven years. The computer-aided design and computer-aided manufacturing (CAD/CAM) project lasts eight years. The advanced computer design project lasts ten.

MCC began operations in September 1983.

Location

The City of Austin, Texas was selected as the home for MCC over Atlanta, San Diego and Research Triangle, North Carolina. A pledge by Texas businessmen to raise $23.5 million in private funding, was a major factor in Austin's selection About $17 million will go to the University of Texas for the construction of the lab building, and equipment, which MCC will lease. Another $5 million will be used for endowed professorships in computer science and engineering. About $1.5 million of the funds will go directly to MCC. It paid for recruitment and relocation expenses, including the lease of a Lear jet.

MCC Organization and Operation

Chairman B. R. Inman has provided several interviews to explain the organization and operation of MCC. Four of these interviews (Refs. 1-4) were provided by MCC for this study. The following items are based on interviews with Adm. Inman and a visit to the MCC Austin headquarters.

- MCC is a direct response to the Japanese success in consumer electronics and computer chip manufacturing, and the ICOT project.
- MCC is directed by a pro-competition initiative, primed to keep a U.S. technological lead. (The current U.S. lead in computer technology has been estimated by Feigenbaum and McCorduck to be two years, but Japan has been gaining at a rate of one day per day.)

- MCC is a for-profit company, with profits to come from royalties earned in licensing. This profit, however, will not come for a long time due to the nature of the research being undertaken.

- The critical difference between MCC and ICOT is that MCC is privately funded by corporations, while ICOT is funded by the Japanese government.

- All of MCC's work is being done in-house.

- Most MCC researchers are from member companies, although a small percentage of technical personnel will come from outside companies.

- MCC is not looking for any Government funding in the next few years, but has not closed the door to that possibility in the future.

- MCC bylaws require that member companies must be at least 50% U.S. owned.

- Noticeably absent from the MCC are IBM, AT&T, Texas Instruments and several other major U.S. corporate leaders. The threat of antitrust problems is the primary reason. IBM declined to seek Justice Department clearance to explore MCC because it viewed the project as competition.

- Each shareholder company can have one liaison person involved in each of the projects it funds. That person shuttles back and forth between the two jobs remaining on the payroll of the shareholder company. MCC reimburses that company for the liaison person's time. The main mission of the technical liaisons is to maintain technical communications between the MCC program and interested organizations within their own company. Shareholders also have the option of sending one or more assigned professionals to apply to project leaders for full-time positions. The position could last from three to five years. At the end of that time, the employee is expected to return to the shareholder company to share the newly acquired technological wealth.

- Each shareholder company can invest money and personnel in any or all of the programs and must commit itself to a minimum of three years of funding for a minimum of one defined project. At present there are six shareholders in microelectronics packaging, six in software, nine in CAD/CAM, and six in advanced computer architectures. Work in all four areas is under the supervision of chief scientist John Pinkston, formerly the deputy director of research at the National Security Agency.

- MCC and the Semiconductor Research Cooperative (SRC) should be cooperative. Some programs overlap, for example both MCC and SRC have programs in CAD/CAM and microelectronics packaging. MCC will tend to pick up where SRC leaves off, turning basic research into advanced development. Several firms are members of both MCC and SRC.

- Whether publication of research results will be allowed is a concern to MCC member companies, since all work is proprietary. No publishing policies have yet been established. It is likely that policies may be similar to those used by Bell Labs.

- MCC is directed with a competition in the international marketplace is healthy, and clearly have not adopted a philosophy that Japan is an adversary, but have a pro-competition initiative aimed at keeping a technological lead.

- MCC has clear guidelines for maintaining confidentiality of research results. All MCC employees sign a proprietary agreement. All intellectual property and patents belong to MCC and employees cannot share them without approval. It is noted that many computer corporations have had problems with the high turnover rate of technical personnel and former employees who start their own ventures. IBM, for example, has made efforts to hold former employees accountable to statements they has signed for protection of proprietary data, and has some lawsuits against people who have moved out and taken ideas with them.

Programs

MCC has four major programs:

- Integrated circuits packaging
- Software technology
- VLSI CAD/CAM
- Advanced computer architectures

The IC packaging program looks at how to accelerate use of gate-array technology in constructing chips and apply that technology to tape-automated-bonding production in a much shorter time.

The software technology program began as a software productivity program. MCC will be looking for near-term productivity enhancements and also totally new ways to engineer software that will allow quantum jumps in the cost of producing software.

The goal in the CAD/CAM program is fabrication of the "one-month chip" -- a system capable of laying out a chip with 10 million transistors in less than a month. It is intended to reduce design costs significantly and to improve engineering productivity.

The 1984 AI/VLSI CAD research computer systems are presented in Figure 1.

The advanced computer-architectures program is substantially the largest, the most expensive, and the longest running. The 10-year program, nicknamed the alpha-omega project, is MCC's "fifth-generation computer" program with the other three contributing to it, as well as standing alone. It will be divided into four areas:

a. Parallel Processing: Develop the the languages and architectures to allow computers to perform tasks simultaneously instead of sequentially, with corresponding increases in processing speed.

b. Database System Management: Improve database design and storage methods and capacities to permit flexible storage and faster retrieval of a broader range of more complex information.

c. Human Factors Technology: Improve the relationship between man and computer, by simplifying the use of computers through techniques such as improved voice or character recognition or use of natural languages.

d. AI/Knowledge Based Systems: Realize the computer's problem solving potential by developing new ways to represent human knowledge and thought concepts, as well as new engineering models and tools to apply human expertise to a wide range of problems.

The first three years will be spend defining what is really known in all of these areas -- where we need additional basic research and where to press on with advanced research. The hope is that VLSI technology will have advanced to a stage by 1987 where it can be applied in all four areas. Defining what it will do, and associated MCC objectives will be a major effort that is probably going to take two or three years. So it will probably be at about the six-year point before MCC starts dealing with the types of designs necessary for computer architectures.

References

1. Fischetti, M. A., "Tomorrow's Computers -- The Quest," IEEE Spectrum, November 1983, pp 54-58.

2. "Talking Shop with Admiral Bobby Inman," Personal Computing, December 1983, pp. 361-387.

3. Steier, Rosalle, "Cooperation Is The Key: An Interview With B. R. Inman," Communications of the ACM, September 1983, pp. 642-645.

- VAX 750 VMS/UNIX
- DEC 2065
- Symbolics 3600
- LMI Lambda
- Texas Instruments Numachine
- Xerox Dandelion
- Sun 120
- Apollo 660

Figure 1. MCC 1984 research computer systems.

4. Johnson, Jan, "America Answers Back," Datamation, May 15, 1984, pp. 40-57.

10

Semiconductor Research Corporation (SRC)

The Semiconductor Research Corporation (SRC) is an organization based in Research Triangle Park, North Carolina, that is implementing an innovative form of industry-university cooperation in research related to plan, promote, coordinate, sponsor, and conduct research that will result in (1) new knowledge of semiconductor materials and phenomena, and of related scientific and engineering subjects that are required for the useful application of semiconductors; (2) the development of new and more efficient design and manufacturing technologies for semiconductor devices; and (3) an increase in the number of scientists and engineers that are proficient in research, development, and manufacture of semiconductor devices. An equally important SRC task is to efficiently communicate the results of its research to its industrial members.

Background

The SRC is a natural derivative of the development of semiconductor technology in the United States The generic technology on which this industry is based was spawned by the Bell Telephone Laboratories in the fifteen years following the invention of the transistor with a major infusion of funding from the defense establishment for research in both industrial and university laboratories. The growth of the semiconductor device industry was so rapid that by the mid-1960s developments within the industry were outpacing the ancillary research community. Both Bell and the Department of Defense (DOD) refocused their efforts to the application of the fruits of their earlier research rather than the continued advancement of the generic technology. Support of academic research shifted in emphasis to longer range, more speculative areas such as compound semiconductors. Research directed to both the near-term and long-range needs of the mainstream semiconductor industry was largely confined to the laboratories of the companies producing the devices. Both merchant producers and the growing number of captive semiconductor producers were involved. These were reluctant to share research results that might provide a competitive advantage. This slowed, but did not stop the diffusion of new results. The research efforts became highly redundant. Each company found it necessary to apply its efforts to very similar topics to avoid being left behind in a critical, rapidly developing technology. Gradually, research became focused on solution of near-term problems, and the generic technology for the longer range future was neglected. Third, and most important, the structure of the industry and the economy resulted in an erosion of the resources available for research, and it was necessary for each company to apply these resources to current product development to remain competitive.

It is important to note that research in compound semiconductors is an important element of the generic technology for future semiconductor products. However, it represents just one of the areas that need to be addressed. It is just as possible that new generations of capabilities may be based on the evolution of silicon technology into radically new device structures as it is possible that new but less developed material systems, such as the III-V semiconductors, will provide these capabilities. Each candidate technology must be addressed in a comprehensive generic technology at a level commensurate with its perceived role.

In late 1981, executives of major United States companies that produce and/or use semiconductor products recognized that this erosion of the generic-technology base coupled with government-financed efforts in other countries constituted an important competitive threat to their industry. Recognizing that a government-based response to this threat was unlikely, they decided to undertake a cooperative industry-initiated response. After considerable discussion, a concept emerged that has become the SRC. This concept is that SRC will:

- Be sponsored by member companies through fees based on semiconductor sales or usage, or semiconductor-related sales.

- Provide knowledgeable and professional planning of an industry-wide research program.

- Contract for research to be coordinated by an industry/SRC technical advisory board.

- Play an active role in monitoring research progress and transferring results back to industry.

- Establish both:

    - University centers of excellence with long-term, major, thrust areas.

    - Additional research activities based on shorter term, more precisely defined objectives.

- The results will be:

    - Establishment of major, focused, generic research program that is supportive of the needs of the semiconductor industry.

    - More relevant graduate education and a larger supply of graduate students.

    - Improved communication within the United States semiconductor community.

Subsidiary research objectives, consistent with these concepts, are to:

- Provide a clearer view of directions, limits, opportunities, and problems in generic technologies.
- Decrease fragmentation and redundancy in United States semiconductor research.
- Establish above-threshold research efforts for critical areas that are beyond the resources of many cooperating companies.
- Enhance the image of the industry in order to attract needed talent.
- Increase industry-university ties.
- Provide a scientific- and technical-information-base for industry development efforts.
- Attract highly qualified students to graduate programs in semiconductor research.
- Help universities to attract and retain competent faculty in semiconductor-related areas.

As part of this set of objectives, it was agreed that the SRC program should encompass universities that are not presently leaders in semiconductor research in order to broaden the institutional base, while increasing the level of effort in universities already active in this technology.

History and Organization

By early 1982, the SRC concept was sufficiently advanced to where, under the aegis of the Semiconductor Industries Association, the SRC was incorporated and by-laws were written. In May 1982, Larry W. Sumney, former director of the DOD Very High Speed Integrated Circuit Program, was hired as Executive Director of the SRC. In September 1982, offices of the SRC were established in the Research Triangle Park of North Carolina, initial staff was hired, and efforts to establish the research program were initiated. By November 1981, contractural procedures were initiated for 8 universities which were selected for award of the first research contracts and 166 proposals were received from 63 universities. By June 1983, over 30 universities were participating in the SRC research program. At this time, the program has expanded to about 40 universities and is operating at a level of nearly $12 million per year.

The SRC exists as a cooperative effort of companies that produce or use semiconductor devices or are major suppliers to the semiconductor industry. Present membership includes:

Advanced Micro Devices, Incorporated
AT&T Technologies, Inc.
Burroughs Corporation
Control Data Corporation
Digital Equipment Corporation
E. I. du Pont de Nemours & Company
Eaton Corporation
E-Systems, Incorporated
GCA Corporation
General Electric Company
General Instrument Corporation
Goodyear Aerospace Corporation
Harris Corporation
Hewlett-Packard Company
Honeywell, Incorporated
IBM Corporation
Intel Corporation
LSI Logic Corporation
Monolithic Memories, Incorporated
Monsanto Company
Motorola, Incorporated
National Semiconductor Corporation
Perkin-Elmer Corporation
RCA Corporation
Rockwell International
SEMI (Chapter)
Silicon Systems, Incorporated
Sperry Corporation
Texas Instruments, Incorporated
Union Carbide Corporation
Varian Associates, Incorporated
Westinghouse Electric Corporation
Xerox Corporation

By the end of 1984, nearly three dozen companies are expected to be members of the SRC and supporting its research activities on the basis of an established fee schedule.

The SRC is operated by a board of directors consisting of 14 members. The board of directors establishes major policy for the SRC, approves major contract awards, approves the appointment of Technical Advisory Board members and key members of the professional staff, and oversees the development and operations of the organization. It is elected annually by the Semiconductor Industry Association (SIA) board.

The Technical Advisory Board has an active role in the evolution of the research program of the SRC participating in the evolution of the research strategy and the evaluation of proposals. It will provide an important conduit for the flow of information from industry to SRC research contracts, and for the flow of research results from the SRC to industry. A full-time SRC staff consists of both regular, permanent employees, and industry personnel assigned to work with the SRC for defined tours of one year or more. This staff, under the direction of the board of directors and with the advice of the Technical Advisory Board, formulates and implements the research program of the SRC. It is intended that the permanent staff remain small so that the active participation of the board of directors, Technical Advisory Board, and industry assignees will continue to be necessary in order to carry out, manage, and direct the SRC program. In addition, it is planned that each contractor will have an industry individual identified as an industry resource contact to provide assistance and information when required.

SRC Mission

In providing its financial support, the semiconductor industry is addressing two objectives: research results, and more university graduates with relevant training. The second objective follows from the first, for SRC research is performed in university laboratories. The SRC's research program involves contracting with universities for research tasks defined and prioritized to be consistent with a research strategy. To assure relevancy, the SRC, working closely with its member companies, has first defined the technology areas of interest and then the technical goals that serve to guide the research toward specific results. Since it is impossible to cover thoroughly all of the required technology, it is necessary to prioritize the candidate areas and allocate funds accordingly. "Research," in this case, must be understood to be the advancement of understanding and the creation of knowledge as opposed to investigations that follow well-defined paths with detailed milestones that leave little of real significance to be discovered.

Program Structure

As of 1 May 1984, the SRC research program reached a level of 53 contracts with 35 universities. Three universities participate in Centers of Excellence; seven in Programs; and the remainder in Projects. Centers of Excellence are so-designated by the board of directors and are recognized as premiere institutions for which the SRC intends to maintain substantial support. Programs are also recognized as commitments to support for extended periods, during which time the quality and productivity of the research is assessed for potential selection as a Center of Excellence. Projects are defined research tasks extending up to 3 years, or beyond, if the requirement persists and the work is outstanding.

The universities in the program structure are:

Centers of Excellence (3)
University of California/Berkeley
Carnegie-Mellon University
Cornell University

Programs (7)
University of California/Santa Barbara
Clemson University
Massachusetts Institute of Technology
University of Michigan
Microelectronics Center of North Carolina
Rensselaer Polytechnic Institute
Stanford University

Projects (28)
University of Arizona
Arizona State University
Brown University
University of California/Los Angeles
Carnegie-Mellon University
Columbia University
Cornell University
University of Florida
Georgia Institute of Technology
University of Illinois/Urbana-Champaign
University of Iowa
The Johns Hopkins University
Massachusetts Institute of Technology
Microelectronics Center of North Carolina
University of Minnesota
Mississippi State University
University of North Carolina/Chapel Hill
University of Notre Dame
The Pennsylvania State University
Purdue University
University of Rochester
University of South Carolina
University of Southern California
Stanford University
The Texas A & M University
University of Vermont
University of Wisconsin
Yale University

Research Program Plan

Before the SRC research program was initiated, a strategy for the program was adopted that identifies the major areas of interest. The major areas identified in this strategy are:

Microstructure Sciences
- Materials, phenomena, and device physics
- Microsciences
- Device fabrication technclogies

Design Sciences
- Design automation
- System - component interactions

Manufacturing System

Automation, robotics
Process modeling and simulation
Packaging
Reliability, quality assurance, and testing

These three programs are summarized in tables I, II, and III.

A three-tier layer of research activities is envisioned consisting of individual project awards, centers of excellence, and lead centers. The first level is intended to comprise those research activities centered around one or several faculty members and their students awarded in a competitive process based on solicitation of proposals for innovative research. The implementation of the first of these solicitations will be described in the next section. At the second level, centers of excellence are being established both through negotiation and competition. These centers will comprise team efforts with themes that can correspond to major areas in the strategy or other mutually acceptable topics that are deemed to be of significant importance. An effort is being made to supplement center themes with research vehicles that provide additional focus to the efforts. The third tier of planned research activity is identified as a lead center and conceptually provides a framework for amalgamating related efforts and facilities of multiple institutions into a structure of coordinated research. The implementation of lead centers will evolve from the present project-center activities at some time in the future.

In addition to the three-tier structure of research described above, an additional program component referred to as a "new thrust" is provided. This is a mechanism for implementation of focused research efforts that respond to needs, opportunities, or technological threats beyond the outlined research strategy. Such efforts will be initiated either through competitive solicitations or from unsolicited proposals. Examples might include areas such as compound semiconductors, high power ICs, novel architectures, electrooptical ICs, or precision processing.

Program Initiation

The initial implementation of the SRC research program was based on a broad solicitation for research proposals that was distributed in September and October of 1982 and on several unsolicited proposals. The competitive solicitation resulted in 166 proposals that were evaluated and ranked in the three major categories of the research strategy. This process resulted in a decision to make awards of approximately 40 contracts to 26 universities. In addition, 37 proposals from 2 universities, RPI and MIT, and one university group, the Microelectronics Center of North Carolina, were removed from the competitive evaluation and are serving as a basis for the establishment of three well-focused research programs. Parallel with this broad

TABLE I
SRC RESEARCH GOALS: MICROSTRUCTURE SCIENCE

- Integratable high-speed logic elements with state discrimination capability in the 5- to 10-femtojoule range
- Compatible interconnection technology
  - Mixed technologies
  - Low-impedance conductors
  - Low-impedance contacts
  - Wafer scale integration
- High-density D-RAM's
- Logic chips with greater than 1-million gate equivalents
- Accurate 16-bit A/D and D/A conversion
- Field-reconfigurable chip technology

TABLE II
SRC RESEARCH GOALS: DESIGN SCIENCES

- Chip functional designs with 10X performance advantages over existing state-of-the-art
- Chip functional designs with reduced interconnection requirements
- Design capabilities at 10 logic element, 10 bit-memory level
- Affordable generic testability methods with 95 percent fault coverage
- Reconfigurable and/or fault tolerant design methodologies
- Hierarchical design systems that require 6 engineering man-months between system specification and error-free layouts

TABLE III
SRC RESEARCH GOALS: MANUFACTURING SCIENCES

- Quality controls that permit production of chips with defect densities below 0.25 cm^3
- Process automation permitting wide product mix from same fabrication lines and a 5X improvement in productivity
- Reduction in fabrication line capital costs for a given production level
- Real-time correlation of process, device, and circuit models in the production environment
- Cost-effective package technologies that extend to:
  - 100 W dissipation
  - High-speed interfaces
  - Optical input/output
  - 400 ports
- Product quality and improvement in chip reliability of 2X without burn-in
- Materials and controls that eliminate yield degradation due to material variables
- Metrology techniques and accuracies that support other manufacturing sciences goals

solicitation, centers of excellence have been established at Cornell University in the area of microscience and technology and at the University of California/Berkeley and Carnegie-Mellon University in computer-aided design.

Future Directions

The innovative character of the SRC and its relative youth limit the precision with which the future course of the organization can be charted. For example, the research emphasis, currently the sole raison d'etre for the SRC, may possibly be altered to include a development thrust. Discussions on the role of the SRC in providing the required bridge from research to application (i.e., development) are taking place, but the nature of this transition organization and the role of the SRC in it have not been decided. It may be that more than one such cooperative development, each with a different focus, may be required.

Within the mainstream research of the SRC, the future will differ in both research and operational characteristics from today's program. Regarding the research characteristics, first, the present program structure predates the definition of research goals. Second, the program balance between technical subject areas is, to some degree, a product of the past conditioning of the university research community by government agencies whose goals are different from those of the SRC. Third, perusal of the present research agenda reveals technical subjects of great importance to future VLSI that are not now being addressed. Last, and most important, in working with its member companies and the universities, the SRC has gained some valuable experience that will be applied in the future. Thus, as the research program progresses, each of the issues will be addressed and, highly dependent on the funding that becomes available, the research agenda will address the full range of VLSI/ULSI needs and opportunities.

Operationally, the SRC future is one of consolidation, assessment, strengthening, and expansion. Consolidation is occurring as membership solicitation activities are phased down and the rate of program expansion becomes necessarily less as the funding levels stabilize. At the same time, the research output of the SRC is increasing, and the electronic linkage to member companies and research participants is coming on line to handle this increased output. Assessments of the research program and of the SRC are being carried out to help shape future courses. Without waiting for the assessment results, improved quality control procedures are being instituted, and the cooperative research concept is being promulgated. The idea that is embodied in this concept is that cooperative research is optimized by providing each participant, member company, university principal investigator, and SRC staff person with full information on the role of each element of the research program, the roles of related elements, and the parameters of the research program so that all cooperators may optimize their actions, thus producing a corporate optimum.

Budget

The 1984 SRC research budget is as follows:

Manufacturing sciences	$ 2,708,580
Design sciences	3,349,988
Microstructure sciences	5,765,040
Annual budget	$11,823,608

SRC centers	$ 3,177,400
SRC projects	4,371,409
SRC programs	4,274,799
Annual budget	$11,823,608

Summary

New efforts are initiated through both competitive and negotiated procurements in specific areas identified by the SRC. The SRC, with a 1984 budget of approximately $13.5 million and a budget of over $16M for 1985, is rapidly establishing a structured research program that responds to the generic technology needs of the integrated circuit industry. Its initial research efforts have focused on addressing nearer-term problems; however, in order to achieve balance and maximize the long-term return-on-investment to its members, the SRC will address the full range of science and technology that will significantly contribute to the advancement of semiconductor technology both in tnis decade and on to the turn of the century. With the support of a growing number of industrial participants, this research will become a major factor in establishing the technology for the information age and will assure the United States industry a position of continued leadership in the semiconductor field as well as in the myriad application areas that depend on advanced semiconductor devices.

11

The Defense Advanced Research Projects Agency (DARPA)

Computing technology already plays an essential role in defense technologies such as guided missiles and munitions, avionics, and C-3I. As new generation technology evolves, there will be unique opportunities for military applications of computing. For example, instead of fielding simple guided missiles or remotely piloted vehicles, completely autonomous land, sea, and air vehicles capable of complex, far-ranging reconnaissance and attack missions might be launched. The possibilities are quite startling, and suggest that new generation computing could fundamentally change the nature of future conflicts. In response to these challenges and opportunities, the Defense Advanced Research Projects Agency (DARPA) has initiated a program in Strategic Computing. To carry out this program, DARPA will fund and coordinate research in industrial, university, and government facilities, and will work with the Military Services and Defense Agencies to insure successful transfer of the results. The overall goal of the program is to create a new generation of machine intelligence technology having unprecedented capabilities and to demonstrate applications of this technology to solving critical problems in Defense. Although the achievements of the program applications' objectives will significantly improve the nation's military capabilities, the impact of nonmilitary spinoffs on the national economy should not be underestimated.

Developing and Demonstrating Applications to Defense

The projections for military applications of new generation computers cover a wide spectrum of activities. They range from applications of individual machines without operators or users as in autonomous systems, to applications involving groups of machines and groups of people collectively engaged in complex tasks as in battle management.

Across this spectrum of applications is a range of requirements for machine-intelligence technology. Some autonomous systems require low-power systems, moderate performance planning and reasoning, and very powerful vision systems. At the other extreme, certain battle management systems will require immense planning and reasoning processors, vast knowledge and data base management systems, perhaps no vision systems, but highly complex distributed, survivable communications systems.

Applications Demonstrations

DARPA has selected three target development projects to demonstrate their research into new generation computing. These projects are:

1. An autonomous vehicle application that will rely heavily on vision and expert system technology.

2. A pilot's associate that exploits speech recognition and expert systems.

3. A battle management system for a carrier battle group that exploits expert system technology and that will eventually exploit very high performance knowledge processing systems.

The following three sections describe these three objective demonstration areas.

Autonomous Vehicles

Autonomous systems are true robotic devices: they are able to sense and interpret their environment, to plan and reason using senses and other data, to initiate actions to be taken, and to communicate with humans or other systems. Examples of autonomous systems include certain "smart" munitions, cruise missiles, various types of vehicles possessing an autonomous navigation capability, and a wide variety of mobile and fixed robotic systems for material handling, manufacturing, and other applications. Some of these systems exist today with operationally useful levels of capability. Others, such as completely autonomous air, land, and undersea vehicles, and systems possessing more adaptive, predatory forms of terminal homing, require the kinds of significant development anticipated in the Strategic Computing program to fully realize their potential. These developments will both enable qualitatively different kinds of autonomous behavior in new systems and effect dramatic quantitative improvements in the operational capabilities of existing systems.

Autonomous vehicles, like other autonomous systems, are characterized by their ability to accept high-level goal statements or task descriptions. For an autonomous vehicle system, one set of goal statements will define a navigation task and another will be specific to its mission, for example reconnaissance. The navigation task will usually be described both in terms of a specific destination for the vehicle and through constraints which limit the number of possible paths or routes the vehicle might use in traversing from one point to another.

Autonomous land vehicle systems, as an example of a class of autonomous vehicles, could support such missions as deep-penetration reconnaissance, rear-area resupply, ammunition handling, and weapons delivery. As an example, imagine a reconnaissance vehicle that could navigate up to 50 km cross-country from one designated position to another. It would be capable of planning an initial route from digital terrain data, updating its plan based on information derived from its sensors, resolving ambiguities between sensed and prestored terrain data, and incorporating landmark prediction and identification as a navigation means. Using advanced image-understanding technology, the reconnaissance payload would perform image segmantation and other basic scene processing upon arrival in a designated area, identify target objects, and report the findings and interpretations.

To develop an autonomous land vehicle with the capavilities described requires an expert system for navigation and a vision system. The expert navigation system must plan routes using digital terrain and environmental data, devise strategies for avoiding unanticipated obstacles, estimate the vehicles' position from landmark and other data, update the onbard digital terrain data base, generate moment-to-moment steering and speed commands, and monitor vehicle performance and onboard systems. All these functions must be accomplished in real-time to near-real-time while the vehicle is moving at speeds up to 60 km/hr. Scaling up from laboratory experiments indicates that such an expert system demonstration would require on the order of 6,500 rules firing at a rate of 7,000 rules/sec. Current systems contain fewer rules, 2,000 on the average, and fire at a rate of 50 to 100 rules/sec. ("Rules" and "firing" are terms used in expert systems. "Rules" represent the codification of an expert system process and "firing" indicates the examination, interpretation, and response to one rule in a particular context. In current systems, the firing of one rule can require the execution of tens of thousands of instructions, and as contexts become more complex the number of instructions for rule-firing increases.)

The vision system must take in data from imaging sensors and interpret these data in real-time to produce a symbolic description of the vehicle's environment. It must recognize roads and road boundaries, select, locate, and dimension fixed and moving obstacles in the roadway, detect, locate, and classify objects in open or forested terrain, locate and identify manmade and natural landmarks, and produce thematic maps of the local environment, while moving at speeds up to 60 km/hr. Scaling-up computing capabilities used in laboratory vision experiments suggests an aggregate computing requirement of 10 to 100 BIPs (billion equivalent von-Neumann instructions per second) to accomplish the above tasks. This compares with capabilities, for example, of 30 to 40 MIPs (million instructions per second) in today's most powerful von-Neumann type computers.

Of equal importance with the required computing capabilities outlined above, is the weight, space, and power required by the computing systems. For a land reconnaissance vehicle, for example, the computers should occupy no more than 6 to 15 ft., weigh less than 200 to 500 lbs., and consume less than 1 kw of power including environmental support. The requirements represent at least 1 to 4 orders of magnitude reduction in weight, space, and power over today's computing systems. For certain space, air, and sea vehicles, the constraints and requirements will be even higher and will include the capability to operate in high-radiation environments.

Pilot's Associate

Pilots in combat are regularly overwhelmed by the quantity of incoming data and communications on which they must base life-or-death decisions. They can be equally overwhelmed by the dozens of switches, buttons, and knobs that cover their control handles demanding precise activation. While each of the aircraft's hundreds of components serve legitimate purposes, the technologies that created them have far outpaced our skill at intelligently interfacing the pilot to them.

This mismatch seems to be characteristic of many human-controlled, complex, dynamic military systems. Further, it applies to single operator as well as to multiple operator situations where crew communication and coordination are essential for survival. It is this type of common military problem that pulls intelligent computing technology into the realm of creating the "personal associate."

The personal associate is viewed as an ensemble of expert-knowledge-based systems and natural interface mechanisms that operate in real-time. In its simplest form, the personal associate performs a set of routine tasks and, when prearranged, initiates actions on its own. In this way, the operator is freed from routine overhead chores and is able to attend to more critical tasks.

In its advanced form, the personal associate performs a set of tasks that are difficult or altogether impossible for the operator, such as the early detection and diagnosis of the subtle patterns of an impending malfunction. In this way, the associate enables completely new capabilities and sophistication.

This concept is illustrated by developing a personal associate within context of combat pilots called the "Pilot's Associate." It is an intelligent system that assists pilots in the air as well as on the ground, not replacing pilots, but by complementing them. The "Pilot's Associate" helps pilots by off-loading lower-level chores and performing special functions so pilots may focus their intellectual resources on tactical and strategic objectives.

The associate is personal to a specific pilot in that it is trained by that pilot to respond in certain ways and to perform particular functions. For example, it might be instructed to automatically reconfigure the aircraft to a specific control sensitivity preferred by the pilot should the wing be damaged during combat. It also has a wealth of general knowledge about the aircraft, the environment, and friendly and hostile forces. It will have instruction on advanced tactics from more experienced pilots and up-to-date intelligence information on enemy tactics to aid less experienced pilots on their first day of combat. These knowledge-bases will be designed for easy updating to keep pace with rapidly changing tactical events. Certain classes of newly "learned" knowledge will be automatically exchanged among pilot's associates.

The approach for this applications is to evolve an increasingly complex pilot's associate in increments that represent key program decision milestones. The development will be continually evaluated in full mission research simulators with representative combat pilots, and eventually moved onboard existing research aircraft for evaluation. The three thrusts central to this development are: the interface to the pilot, the knowledge-bases to support the interface, and integration and interpretation processors that connect these.

The interface is based upon natural communication using advances in speech recognition (developed here for the noisy, stressful cockpit environment), speech output (particularly machine speech that can assume different speaker types and styles), and graphic or pictorial presentation of complicated information.

Knowledge-bases will be developed that are significantly larger than any previously attempted. For example, the simple monitoring of the basic flight systems (power, electrical, and hydraulic) could take several thousand rules. These will have to be processed at rates perhaps 100 times faster than the current technology allows. The knowledge-bases that will be developed are:

- The aircraft/pilot
- Tactics and strategy
- Enemy aircraft
- Communication
- Geography
- Navigation aids
- The mission
- Enemy defense
- Friendly forces

The processes that integrate and interpret the demands from the interface with the contents of the knowledge-bases include functions that tie flight events to the mission plan prepared earlier, change environmental and threat situations, coordinate with other pilot's associates in the air and on the ground, continually change situational-data bases for local battles as they develop, and so forth.

Eventually, the demand for real time processing in small, rugged packages for onboard installation characterizes the "pull" that this application puts on the Strategic Computing program. The knowledge gained will directly complement important service research programs such as the USAF Cockpit Automation Technology effort.

Battle Management

Management of large-scale enterprises is characterized by decisionmaking under uncertainty. The system must alert the decisionmaker to the existence of an incipient problem, generate potential responses to the problem in the form of decision options, evaluate these options in the face of uncertainty about the outcome arising from any specific option and with respect to often conflicting goals, execute the preferred option, and monitor its execution, iterating on the above process as circumstances dictate. No examples exist today of systems that directly address each of the above steps. While many individual information processing systems, such as the World Wide Military Command and Control System (WWMCCS) and various intelligence systems, furnish data to the decision maker that support such functions as alerting and option generating, the fact remains that no systems exist which directly aid such cognitive processes as option generation, uncertainty assessment, and multiattribute value reconciliation. These are knowledge intensive and the development of aids in these and other critical areas will consequently require the kinds of expert system and natural language developments anticipated from the Strategic Computing Program.

An example of a system that would aid in the management of a large enterprise, a battle management system (BMS) would interact with the user at a high level through speech and natural language. It would be capable of comprehending uncertain data to produce forecasts of likely events, drawing on previous human and machine experience to generate potential courses of action, evaluating these options and explaining the supporting rationale for the evaluations to the decisionmaker, developing a plan for implementing the option selected by the decisionmaker, disseminating this plan to those concerned, and reporting progress to the decisionmaker during the execution phase.

For example, a battle management system for a carrier battle group would be integrated into the Composite Warfare Commander (CWC) battle group defense system. It would display a detailed picture of the battle area, including enemy order of battle (surface, air, subsurface), own force disposition, electronic warfare environment, strike plan, weather forecast, and other factors developed from an analysis of all available data. It would generate hypotheses describing possible enemy intent, prioritize these according to their induced likelihood, and explain the reasons for the prioritization. Drawing upon previous experience, together with knowledge of own force and enemy capabilities, it would generate potential courses of action, use an ultrarapid rule-based simulation to project and explain a likely outcome for each course of action, and evaluate and explain the relative attractiveness of each outcome considering such criteria as protection of own forces, inflicting damage on the enemy, and the rules of engagement. Once the commander selects a course of action, the BMS would prepare and disseminate the operation plan (OPLAN), and compare the effects of option execution with those developed through the simulation, both as a check on progress and as a means of identifying the need to replan. At the conclusion of every phase of the engagement, the BMS would modify its expert system in the light of empirical results.

To realize the capabilities described above will require the development of a number of expert systems and a natural language interface. The expert systems for the demonstration BMS will make inferences about enemy and own-force air order-of-battle that explicitly include uncertainty, generate strike options, carry out simulations for evaluating these strike options, generate the OPLAN, and produce explanations. It is estimated that in the aggregate, the above functions define a distributed expert system requiring some 20,000 rules and processing speeds of 10 BIPs. The natural language system alone will require a processing speed of 10 BIPs. The natural language system alone will require a processing speed of about 1 BIP.

Space-based signal processing requirements for surveillance and communications will require low power, very high speed, radiation-hardened, integrated circuits based on gallium-arsenide technology. These circuits will operate at speeds of at least 200 MHz, with tens of milliwatts of power required for a typical 16 kilobit memory, in radiation up to 5 x 10 to the 7 power rads.

New Computing Technology

Several specific technology areas will have to be advanced to meet the objectives of the DARPA program. The primary areas targeted to basic research are:

1. Vision
2. Speech recognition and production
3. Natural language understanding
4. Expert systems
5. Hardware/software system architecture
6. Signal processing
7. Symbolic processing
8. Multifunction machines
9. Silicon technology
10. GaAs pilot lines
11. Memory technology
12. High performance technology

The following sections describe developmental requirements in these areas.

Vision

Computer vision, also called "image understanding," is the information-processing task of comprehending a scene from its projected image. It differs from related disciplines such as pattern recognition and image processing in that the process of image understanding builds a description not only of the image data itself, but also of the actual scene that is depicted. Image understanding requires knowledge about the task world, as well as sophisticated image-processing techniques.

DARPA has carried on a basic research program in computer vision for some years. The technology has matured to the point where it can not be exploited in meaningful ways. Since the autonomous vehicle application described previously stresses the technology development to a significant extent, it will serve as the initial driver of technology research. In order to meet objectives of the vehicle application, generic recognition capability will be required for both vehicle navigation and for reconnaissance. A vision subsystem will have to provide for the recognition and identification of obstacles that might deter local navigation and also for landmarks that can be used to fix vehicle position in the global navigational sense. The vision component must also be able to recognize targets and understand, at least from the standpoint of threat evaluation, what is happening to objects of interest from scene to scene. To achieve these capabilities, specific advances will have to be made in vision software and in the hardware that will run the necessary computer programs.

There currently exist software algorithms that perform object recognition in highly specific task domains, but techniques will have to be developed that generalize this capability. Furthermore, the recognition process will have to be robust enough to permit recognition in the face of occlusion, shadows, and differing orientations. The key to achieving this capability is significant advances in high-level modeling and use for knowledge-based recognition techniques. These concerns will receive strong emphasis in the early stages of the project. There will also be efforts to implement discrimination capabilities to differentiate objects of interest, e.g., discerning obstacles as opposed to landmarks or targets. As the system evolves, it should also develop the capacity to detect moving objects within its range of vision, understand that they are moving, and comprehend the relations of their movement to other objects in the scene.

Recent progress in developing vision for navigation has been severely constrained by lack of adequate computing hardware. Not only are the machines that are now being used too large to be carried by the experimental vehicles, but current machines are far too slow to execute the vision algorithms in real-time. For example, in an experimental university research program, a "corridor rover" applied a vision subsystem to navigate itself down corridors that had various obstacles in its path. The scene is reanalyzed after the cart has moved 1 meter. The current algorithms require 15 minutes of computer time for each meter moved. If the vehicle were moved at a walking pace, the computing requirements would be about 3 orders of magnitude greater. Future applications will have more complex scenes, be required to move faster, and also require the performance of various tasks enroute.

It is estimated that 1 trillion von Neumann equivalent computer operations per second are required to perform the vehicle vision task at a level that will satisfy the autonomous vehicle project's long-range objectives. At best, current machines of reasonable cost achieve processing rates below 100 million operations per second. The required factor of 10 to the 6 power improvement in speed will have to be achieved through VLSI implementation of massively parallel architectures. In order to make use of these architectures, parallel algorithms will have to be developed. Therefore, part of the early research efforts will also concentrate on the development of suitable parallel algorithms. It is felt that low-level vision processes can be exploited in a more straightforward fashion because of the inherent parallel nature of images and the local operations that are performed. Thus, initial emphasis will concentrate on algorithms at this level. The parallel programming efforts will evolve to embrace the higher-level vision processes as a better understanding of the problems is gained .

The most significant technology that will result from this effort is a generic scene understanding capability. This technology will be exportable to a wide range of military applications, including cruise missile enroute navigation and terminal homing, as well as to a wide variety of fire-and-forget weaponry.

Functional Objectives for Vision Subsystems

FY 86 Model and recognize simple terrain with crude objects
FY 88 Recognize and match landmarks with maps in simple terrain
FY 90 Recognize and match landmarks with obstacles in complex terrain using rich object descriptions
FY 92 Perform reconnaissance in a dynamically changing environment

Speech Recognition and Production

The program goal for speech subsystems is to enable real-time speech input to computers and the generation of meaningful acoustic output. Past efforts in speech understanding have been limited by both inadequate processing capabilities and by an inadequate understanding of the acoustic phonetics of speech. Ongoing basic research programs in speech are addressing a number of the basic issues. This program will capitalize on the results of this basic research.

The capabilities of a speech subsystem vary along several dimensions that include:

- isolated word recognition to continuous speech
- speaker-dependent to speaker independent.
- quiet environments to noise, stressful environments
- small vocabularies in limited context to vocabularies having 10,000 or more words

This program is concentrating on developing speech recognition and generating high-performance capabilities for two generic types of applications: one in a high-noise, stress environment, where a limited vocabulary can be useful, such as in the fighter cockpit, and another in a moderate-noise environment where a very large vocabulary is required, such as in a battle management system. The technology is applicable to many other tasks; the applications cited here provide a focus for the research and insure that these specific applications will be supported with speech.

For the cockpit application, the major challenge will be to develop speech recognition algorithms that can operate in a fighter aircraft environment. This includes noise levels up to 155 dB, acceleration to several gs, voice distortions due to the helmet and facemask, and changing voice characteristics under the stresses of combat. The initial computational requirements are estimated to be 40 MIPs to demonstrate speech recognition in the cockpit, counting both the signal processing and recognition functions. Furthermore, this hardware must be sufficiently compact so it does not exceed the restricted space and power that is available in a fighter aircraft.

The initial set of tasks focuses on speaker-dependent isolated word recognition in a noisy environment. The specific use of speech recognition in the cockpit needs to be studied in detail to understand which tasks should be performed by voice, how voice will impact other systems, what vocabulary is needed, etc. Speaker-dependent algorithms for recognizing words in a noise environment will be developed initially, and will later be extended to speaker-independent algorithms. A prototype architecture for performing the real-time recognition tasks will be developed and used to evaluate algorithms in a simulated cockpit environment. This initial architecture would be composed of off-the-shelf hardware and would not be suitable for flight. Compact hardware will be developed, including custom hardware for performing computer-intensive functions such as template matching.

Support of spoken natural language input and output for a battle management system will require real-time continuous speech recognition and generation of very large vocabularies of 1,000 to 10,000 words with natural syntax and semantics, in a relatively benign acoustic environment. Techniques will need to be developed for the acquisition and representation of knowledge of speech variability due to alternate pronunciations, context in continuous speech, and different speakers. Efficient parallel search algorithms and hardware, combined with techniques for focusing attention on key words, will be developed for dealing with large vocabularies. Automated techniques will be developed for acquiring the acoustic, syntactic, and semantic knowledge to switch among multiple-task domains. Advanced acoustic-phonetic algorithms will be needed to distinguish among similar words in large vocabularies. Integration of the speech system with the natural language system will be required to perform the overall battle management task.

Increasing speech capabilities will be developed over time, with an initial goal of a 1,000-word speaker-adaptive system, and an ultimate goal of a 10,000-word speaker-independent system. It is estimated that the computational requirements of the latter system will be on the order of 20 BIPs.

Functional Objectives for Speech Subsystems

FY 86 Recognition of words from a 100-word vocabulary for a given speaker under severe noise and moderate stress conditions

FY 88 Recognition of sentences from a 1,000-word vocabulary with moderate grammatical constraints in a speaker adaptive mode under low noise and stress conditions

FY 89 Recognition of connected speech, independent of speakers from a 200-word vocabulary with strict grammatical constraints under severe noise and high stress conditions

FY 92 Recognition of sentences, independent of speakers, from a 10,000-word vocabulary with natural grammar under moderate noise and low stress conditions

Natural Language Understanding

The most common way for people to communicate is by expressing themselves in a natural language such as English. If DARPA can produce computer programs that can deal with a substantial subset of English meaning, they make headway on several fronts. They could provide natural language interfaces so that tactical experts can be closely coupled with supporting data bases and automated expert systems. Such interfaces would accept data inputs, commands, and queries in natural language and could furnish responses either in natural language or in the form of easily understandable text and tables. They could also develop systems that understand streams of text to achieve automatic input of information transmitted in that form.

Natural language research has matured to the point where it is finding applications as a human-machine interface in various commercial equipments. However, its application to operational military environments is still limited by the lack of sufficient computing capacity, an inadequate understanding of semantics and discourse context, inadequate vocabularies, and the conceptually challenging and time-consuming problem of introducing sufficient knowledge and semantics into the system. Ongoing basic research programs will address some of these issues and feed into this program but additional intensive efforts are needed to achieve the technology-level necessary for meeting the requirements of the battle management application described elsewhere in this plan.

The technology subprogram in natural language has the overall objective of achieving an automated understanding and generation capability that can be used in a variety of applications. DARPA will undertake research that supports this objective by focusing on the technology needed to fulfill the specific natural language requirements of the battle management problem. This approach will not only support the implementation of a battle management system, but progress made in this area will also be applicable to a wide class of similar problems. Meeting the requirements will entail the development of a highly intelligent natural language interface between the user and the machine. In addition, a text processing component will be developed that can classify text by its context, determine and store the key events, and retrieve the relevant information by contextual reference with an accuracy of no less than 95%.

In order to achieve the desired capability of the natural language front end, it will be necessary to make significant advances in three specific areas. First, natural language understanding programs must have a much greater comprehension of the context of the ongoing discourse between the user and the machine. This will insignificantly reduce the amount of dialogue that has to take place by instilling the capability within the machine to anticipate requirements of the user. Second, a much more sophisticated level of natural language response on the part of the machine is required so that information can be presented in the most meaningful way to the user. Third, an interactive facility for the acquisition of knowledge has to be developed. This is driven by the time-consuming requirements of incorporating new linguistic and semantic knowledge in the system. In the area of text understanding, advances must be made in the area of cognitive memory modeling and text comprehension.

In order to develop the targeted capability, several milestone systems will be built. The first of these will integrate and slightly extend existing natural language interface techniques. There will then be a dual effort, one aimed at text processing and the other at interactive dialogue systems. Each of these efforts will result in specialized intermediate milestone systems. Finally, these streams will be joined together to achieve the full functional capability necessary to support the battle management application.

Functional Objectives for Natural Language Subsystems

- FY 86 Natural language interfaces with some understanding of commands, data inputs, and queries (e.g., interfact to a data base and a threat-assessment expert system)
- FY 88 Domain-specific text understanding (e.g., understand paragraph-length intelligence material relating to air threat)
- FY 90 Interactive planning assistant that carries on task-oriented conversation with the user
- FY 93 Interactive, multiuser acquisition, analysis, and explanation system that provides planning support and substantive understanding of streams of textual information

The tasks described above will require substantially larger vocabularies that are currently available and significant gains in processing power to accomplish understanding and response in real-time. It is estimated that vocabularies of 15,000 words and processing speeds of 1 billion operations per second will be needed to achieve this goal. In addition, to be useful for practical applications, this power must come in compact dimensions. These constraints will generally necessitate the utilization of massively parallel VLSI computational devices. Such an architecture will, in turn, demand the reformulation and development of parallel algorithms for natural language understanding.

Expert System Technology

Expert system technology has matured to become a highly exploitable application area of the science of artificial intelligence. It is characterized by the explicit use of specific domain knowledge (usually gleaned from human experts) to develop computer systems that can solve complex, real-world problems of military, scientific, engineering, medical, and management specialists.

Examples of successful applications include programs to perform electronic warfare signal analysis, medical diagnosis, geological evaluation of designated sites, oil well dipmeter analysis, maintenance of locomotives, and carrier air operations. It is a technology that is most appropriate for command and control operations, situation assessment, and high-level planning. Thus, it will play a vital role in the military applications examples described elsewhere in this plan.

Expert system technology has evolved to a point where a variety of general purpose inferencing and reasoning systems are available. These systems can be augmented with specific domain knowledge to prepare them for particular applications. Currently, the most time consuming portion of the process of constructing the expert system is the articulation of knowledge by the expert and its satisfactory formulation in a suitable knowledge-representation language for mechanization by computer.

There are many opportunities for dramatic advances in the technology. These include advances in explanation and presentation capability, improved ability to handle uncertain and missing knowledge and data, more flexible control mechanisms, expansion of knowledge capacity and extent, enhanced inference capability (in terms of speed, flexibility, and power), development of intersystem cooperation, and improvement of software support tools. Intensive development attention devoted to these issues can be expected to lead to important applications of expert systems in complex military environments.

The Strategic Computing expert system technology effort will exploit these opportunities by generating and extending AI techniques, by improving software support tools, and by using specialized symbolic computational hardware. Work in representation will build toward a capability for large (30,000 rule) knowledge bases. Inference techniques will be extended to handle these knowledge bases even when they contain uncertain knowledge and must operate on flawed and incomplete data. Explanation and presentation systems, ultimately using a 10,000 word speech-understanding system, will allow verbal inputs from (and discussions with) the user about the systems' assessments, recommendations, and plans. The knowledge acquisition work will focus on developing facilities for automated input of domain knowledge directly from experts, text, and data. Software support efforts will lead to a progression of increasingly powerful expert system workstations to be used in developing the needed technology.

The achievement of these complex capabilities will severely tax computational resources so that significant gains in processing power will be required to perform in real time or in simulations faster than real time. It is estimated that hybrid expert system architectural configurations will be required that can accommodate 30,000 rules and perform at a capacity of 12,000 rules per real-time second at rates up to 5 times real time. Due to compact size and cost constraints, it is anticipated that this architecture will be realized through VLSI devices incorporating massive parallelism, active semantic memories, and specialized inference mechanisms. Such configurations will require significant efforts to develop the algorithms required for parallel execution. It should be noted that the rules per second quantifications are subject to many factors, and are for comparison purposes only. Rules applied in applications late in the program will be more complex than present ones, and their contexts for firing will be vastly more complex than those common in present-day expert systems.

The results of this effort will specifically support the goals of the three example military applications. However, the resulting technology will be substantially generic in nature so that it will significantly advance expert systems capabilities and support a wide range of applications for both the government and industry.

Hardware/Software System Architecture and Design

Most of today's computers are still single-processor von Neumann machines, and the few efforts to build commercial multiprocessor systems have yielded systems containing only a few processors (generally less than 10). The underlying electronic circuit technology is advancing at a rate that will provide a speed improvement factor of only 20 to 30% per year, at most, for such machines. For future computer systems to have substantially greater power, they must rely heavily on parallelism. While many ideas have been developed for algorithms, languages, and system software for high performance parallel machines, practical experience with actual experimental parallel systems is still very limited, and must be greatly expanded.

Greater computing power can also be achieved through specialization of machines to particular computing functions. Such specialized machines exhibit exceptional performance, but only on the class of problems for which they were designed. Parallelism is a form of specialization of a machine to a class of problems. For example, array processors will outperform a comparably priced general purpose computer by factors of 10 to 100 on linear algebra, finite element analysis, and similar problems. Future high-performance systems for applications such as the control of autonomous vehicles must support a diverse and demanding set of functions with high reliability. Such systems will be composed of a variety of modules configured to perform many specialized functions efficiently, in parallel, and with reduncancy appropriate to the application. For example, the control of autonomous vehicles may employ modules specialized in signal processing to handle the image processing at the lowest level, modules specialized in pattern matching to handle the scene analysis, and other modules to handle cognitive functions, control, and communications. This integration of diverse machines into complete systems depends on standardization of hardware, software, and network interfaces.

Computer architecture is concerned with the structures by which memories, processing nodes, and peripherals are interconnected; the computational capabilities of the processing nodes; and the software which is required to exploit the hardware. Ideas have been proposed for machines which are interconnected in a variety of ways, and given descriptive names such as Boolean n-cubes, trees, perfect shuffles, and meshes. Processor nodes have been proposed that are designed for floating point operations, search operations, logic operations, etc., and language and operating system concepts have been proposed for exploiting parallelism. It is from this collection of ideas that specific architectures have been proposed, and in some cases, simulated or constructed on a very small scale.

To understand the capabilities and limitations of a proposed architecture, a prototype of the machine must be simulated or built, software must be developed, and the system evaluated on a class of problems for which the machine was designed. The role of software cannot be overemphasized. Existing languages are generally not applicable for highly parallel architectures. Special compilers are needed, as are debugging tools and tools to measure the performance of the resulting system. In evaluating a new architecture, it is more important to initially understand the applicability of the architecture to an important class of problems than to strive for high performance in a prototype implementation. Thus, to know that a 100-processor system gives a 50'-fold increase over a single node of that system is more important than knowing the maximum instruction rate that can be executed or knowing the exact instruction rate achieved with prototype hardware. Once a prototype machine has proven to be promising, higher performance versions can be built by using faster components and by scaling the entire system to have more processors.

This program will develop and evaluate new architectures in three broad areas: signal processing, symbolic processing, and multifunction machines. These classes of machines are described below, along with the development plans for each class. In general, several prototype systems will be developed in the early phase of the program. An evaluation phase will permit different architectural approaches to be compared. DARPA will select from the different prototypes those that are most successful and that will be continued to develop high-performance versions.

Signal Processing

An important class of applications known as signal processing involves taking real-time data from a sensor and performing a series of operations on each data element. These operations might involve transformations such as an FFT, correlations, filtering, etc., and are dominated by performing multiplications and additions. High data rates are common, and computation rates in excess of 1 billion operations/sec are needed. Military applications of such signal processing include processing data from radar, sonar, infrared sensors, images, and speech.

The exploitation of parallelism in signal processing will be based on the use of computational arrays such as systolic arrays, in which many simple, highly regular processing elements "pump" data from cell to cell in a "wavelike" motion to perform the successive operations on each element of data. An architecture based on this concept will be developed, with the goal of building a system capable of executing 1 billion or more operations/sec by 1986. Other concepts that exploit signal-processing data regularity will also be investigated. By the end of the decade, the goal is to develop a system capable of 1 trillion operations/sec.

The software support, and programming languages for the signal processing system will be developed in parallel with the hardware. Most of the initial programming for the prototype system will be done at the microcode level. The requirements for operating system, programming languages and programming environments will be developed as experience is gained using the prototype systems.

Symbolic Processing

Symbolic processing deals with nonnumeric objects, relationships among these objects, and the ability to infer or deduce new information with the aid of programs that "reason." Examples of symbolic computation include searching and comparing complex structures (e.g., partial pattern matching). Applications that make extensive use of symbolic computing include vision systems that can tell what is in a scene, natural language systems that can "understand" the meaning of an English sentence, speech-understanding systems that can recognize spoken words, and planning systems that can provide intelligent advice to a decisionmaker. Most programs that perform symbolic processing are now written in the language called LISP. Special machines, called LISP machines, are now available commercially and offer computing rates in excess of one MIP. Further development of these conventional uniprocessor LISP machines will take place under the technology infrastructure portion of the program. An ultimate performance improvement of about 50 times the current level can be achieved with these conventional techniques and the use of advanced technology.

Current applications in areas such as vision now require about three orders of magnitude more processing than is now available. As future algorithms and applications are developed, even more computing power will be necessary.

The symbolic processors of the future may well be a collection of special components that are interconnected via a general purpose host computer or by high-speed networks. Based on software systems that have been developed for applications in vision, natural language, expert systems, and speech, several of these components have been identified. As much as four orders of magnitude speedup may be available by taking advantage of the parallelism in some of these specific areas. Some of the components include the following:

- A semantic memory subsystem -- used to represent knowledge relating concepts to other concepts in natural language, speech understanding, and planning domains.

- A signal-to-symbol transducer -- used to make the initial step in extracting meaning from low-level signal processing computations (e.g., phonetic classification, or object identification from boundary information).

- A production rule subsystem -- a system that combines knowledge and precedures for problem-solving. A system now aboard the carrier Carl Vinson uses this approach.

- A fusion subsystem -- a method for permitting multiple sources of information to share their knowledge. It is used to "fuse" information in tasks such as battle management.

- An inferencing subsystem -- a system that uses first order formal logic to perform reasoning and theorem proving.

- A search subsystem -- a mechanism that explores numerous hypotheses, pruning these intelligently to determine likely candidates for futher symbolic processing.

The program will consist of three phases. Phase I concentrates on architecture design, simulation, algorithm analysis, and benchmark development for promising architectural ideas such as those described above. It will also include the development and initial evaluation of the unique integrated components necessary for the implementation of these architectures. The design of concurrent LISP-like languages for programming these machines will also be addressed.

Existing high-performance scientific computers such as the Cray-1, CDC 205, Denelcor HEP, and the S-1 will be benchmarked using a portable LISP computer to determine their relative abilities to handle symbolic computation.

Phase II will engineer full-scale prototype versions of selected architectures, supporting these hardware developments with extensive diagnostic and compilation tools. The goal of this phase is implementation of a specific target problem on each of the selected architectures for benchmarking purposes.

Phase III will integrate developments of the signal processing, symbolic, and multifunction development efforts into a composite system capable of addressing a significant problem domain. Such a system for the control of an autonomous vehicle, for example, might include a high-performance vision processing front-end based on the the computational array technology, a signal-to-symbol transformer for classifying objects, a fusion subsystem for integration information from multiple sources, an inferencing engine for reasoning and top-level control, and a multifunction processor for controlling the manipulator effectors. This phase will also pursue higher performance versions of selected machines.

Multifunction Machines

A multifunction machine is capable of executing a wider range of different types of computations than the more specialized machines described above, but at possible lower performance in the specialized machine's application domain. These multifunction machines achieve high performance with parallelism. DARPA aims to develop machines of this class having 1000 processors. The processing elements in a multifunction machine would typically be general purpose processors or computers. These elements communicate either through shared storage or networks with such interconnection strategies as rings, trees, Boolean n-cubes, perfect shuffle networks, lattices, or meshes.

About 6 to 8 prototype multifunction systems will be developed, based on custom VLSI chips, commercial microprocessor chips, or commercial processors. These systems will be benchmarked to determine how different hardware architectures and programming strategies scale in performance. Subsequently, two or three such systems will be selected in this evaluation process for continued development for advanced technology versions and production quality software.

Central to this program is the development of programming models and methods which will permit the convenient development of new classes of algorithms that will contain very high levels of concurrency. The way in which concurrency manifests itself in program structures can be viewed as resulting from the linguistic control methods of the programming language in which the program is written. Examples of control models that will be investigated are the control-driven, data-driven, and demand-driven styles. Control-driven concurrent programming models are already evolving from existing programming languages. Examples are concurrent PASCAL, parallel LISP, etc. In this model, program actions are sequenced by explicit control mechanisms such as CALL, JUMP, or PARBEGIN. In the data-driven model, program actions are driven into activity by the arrival of the requisite operand set. The advantage of this style is that concurrency can often be specified implicitly. The demand-driven model is based on the propagation of demands for results to invoke actions. This style has been successfully employed for parallel evaluation of LISP code. In this scheme, concurrent demands are propagated for argument evaluation of LISP functions. It is likely that new or possibly composite models such as concurrent-object oriented programming will surface, but it is also likely that advances in each area will provide highly concurrent program-based solutions for many application areas.

An important part of this project will be the implementation of new concurrent programming languages which exploit these models. The language development will need to be coupled with programming environment tools and compatible hardware and operating system software. This development will provide the necessary computational tools to support application studies aimed at the creation of highly parallel application programs that can take advantage of the large levels of concurrency provided by multifunction machine prototypes. The long-term goal of this research is ultraspeed, cost-effective demonstrations of important application areas such as data base access, system simulation, and physical modeling.

Given a particular instance of machine and a particular parallel program, the remaining issue is how the program should be mapped onto the physical resources in order to permit efficient exploitation of concurrency. This resource allocation problem is one of the key technical issues addressed by this program. There are two styles usually employed in the solution of this problem: static allocation and dynamic allocation.

In a static mapping strategy, the concurrency structure of the program is evaluated with respect to the topology of the physical machine. The compiler can then create specific load modules for the physical nodes of the target machine. This static method is simpler than the dynamic method but needs to be developed for each of the architectures that are being pursued. If the number of components is very large, then it is likely that component failures will occur. With the static allocation mechanism, it will be necessary to recompile the program for the current machine configuration.

In a dynamic allocation strategy, it is still important for the compiler to do some of the allocation task collection but the output of the compiler is not in the form of specific load modules. Dynamic strategies allow the loader to define the final physical target of a compiled module based on hardware availability. Another extension to the dynamic strategy is to additionally move tasks around to balance system load. An important byproduct of this program will be the development and implementation of both static and dynamic allocation strategies but it is expected that acceptable static allocations methods will precede the more sophisticated dynamic strategies.

Supporting Microelectronics Technology

Computing technology relies heavily on microelectronics in order to achieve systems capabilities while meeting critical constraints on such factors as size, weight, power dissipation, and operating environments. Microelectronics provides computing systems with required integration complexity, switching speed, switching energy, and tolerance to hostile environments. In the case of military systems, special emphasis must be given to survival in radiation environments. Microelectronic packaging and interconnect technologies provide additional important support in meeting system constraints.

This program will place strong emphasis on the effective exploitation of such microelectronic technology. A key concept that will be used to exploit state-of-the-art microelectronics is to dramatically reduce the usual longtime delays between basic research innovations in fabrication and packaging technology and their subsequent exploitation by designers. This will be done by creating a pilot line(s) for the particular technology and at the same time creating the associated designer-to-implementation system-to-foundry interfaces (design rules, process test inserts, design examples, design libraries, implementation system protocols, etc.). Once a new technology has been demonstrated as feasible and stable in pilot-line form, it may then be selected for inclusion in program infrastructure.

Silicon Technology

Silicon technology will be the mainstay of this program because of its maturity and its accessibility through existing infrastructure. Early versions of the proposed subsystems prototypes will use the 3 x 10-11 gate hertz/cm^2 technologies made possible by VLSI/VHSIC. More advanced technologies such as the VHSIC Phase II will also be utilized as they become available. For subsystems or systems that require even greater throughput this program will competitively purchase wafer-level integration technology from emerging sources. This will result in the gain of at least another order of magnitude in the computational throughput of a monolithic chip and an equally significant reduction in power consumption for a given operation by diminishing the number of required off-chip drives.

Even such gains will not fulfill the ultimate weight, volume, and speed requirements of such systems as certain autonomous vehicles that will require better than 10-10 operations per second and 10-11 bits of memory in less than a few cubic feet using no more than a kilowatt of power. For these requirements to be met, new fabrication technology must be developed yielding devices an order of magnitude smaller than those produced today. Ultimately, techniques now in basic research phases such a ion-beam processing technology, laser processing and X-ray lithography may be combined with silicon molecular bean epitaxy into a pilot-line system capable of growing multiple semiconductor and insulator layers, adding localized ion doping, etching via holes, and depositing interconnect metal. If successful in moving from basic research, such efforts could eventually reduce from month to days the time required to fabricate prototype custom circuits of high complexity.

GaAs Pilot Lines

Survivable, space-based electornics will require the two orders of magnitude increased total dose radiation tolerance that is inherent to GaAs-based microelectronics technologies. The establishment of pilot lines, running at a throughput of at least 100 wafers per week, will place, for the first time, the production rigor on the fabrication of GaAs-integrated circuits necessary to achieve acceptable yields and make GaAs circuits affordable to the military. The GaAs pilot lines will be producing low-power, radiation-hard memory and logic chips as fundamental building blocks for radiation-hardened systems. Communication and surveillance systems that can survive in a strategic conflict are important components of a space-based battle management system. In addition to the primary advantage of high-radiation tolerance, GaAs-based microelectronics will also produce circuits with larger operating temperature range, both lower and higher than silicon, and faster on-chip switching speed at a given power level.

Memory Technology

Rapid-access, low-power memory subsystems that can be operated in the field and powered from conventional sources are needed by many applications. Today's largest disk storage systems contain on the order of a gigabyte of memory but are too large and power-consuming for use in the field. Progress must be made in both size and power reduction. Systems needs for as large as 100 gigabyte memories with rapid access are envisioned for autonomous systems. The program will capitalize on progress in industry and in other basic research programs.

High Performance Technology

The need to increase system computational speeds may be met by using fabrication technology that can tailor material properties by creating artificial compounds and superlattices of differing materials (for example, by using Molecular Beam Epitaxy [MBE] technology). Successful pilot-lining of MBE would contribute to conventional microelectronics, microelectronics with optoelectronic I/O, and eventually to massively parallel computations using optical computing elements. When available, optoelectronic interconnect technology will allow the number of cables and the power dissipation in large multiprocessor systems to be reduced dramatically.

As Molecular Beam Epitaxy (MBE) systems advance into a practical production tool, heterostructure devices can be fabricated to produce high frequency devices. Such a development could reduce transmit-receive satellite systems, presently requiring 6-ft dishes, to handheld devices by utilizing the 94 GHz atmospheric window. Such systems will contribute in a revolutionary manner to size, weight, and cost of battle management communications subsystems.

Advanced computing subsystems-on-a-chip will require both high speed and high pin-count packages. The VHSIC program is developing 250 pin packages, but these are only suitable up to a 40 MHz clock rate. This program will initiate development and/or compete the selection of large pin-count packages, including those that employ microwave signal propagation principles. Longer term efforts directed toward achieving (optoelectronic) packages required to handle broad band operation from d.c. to multigigahertz, with up to 200 signal lines in addition to power and ground leads will be factored into the program where appropriate.

12

European Strategic Program of Research and Development in Information Technology (ESPRIT)

The European Economic Community has launched the European Strategic Program of Research and Development in Information Technology (ESPRIT). ESPRIT is intended to promote precompetitive and generic research and development in information technology through collaborative projects within the European community which the community shall finance in part. Specific objectives are to:

- Promote European industrial cooperation in precompetitive R&D in Information Technology

- Provide European Information Technology industry with the basic technologies it needs to be competitive on the world market in 5 to 10 years

- Pave the way for standards

Specifically, the goals of ESPRIT encompass:

- A new level of man-machine interfaces so that the user will feel more at home and can communicate in more "natural" ways. Machines will have to understand natural language, whether spoken or handwritten.

- A greater degree of interactivity that will allow the machine greater leeway or delegation to solve problems. Thus a system should become more "intelligent" and begin to fill out the details itself. It may find ambiguities and contradictions in the desires of the user and begin a dialogue to resolve them.

- The system will need to understand more about the background to a problem so that it can both explain its conclusion and also what it will do further if the result is unsatisfactory to the user.

- Integration of various services and functions will require interconnected local- and wide-area networks and all possible forms of distributed processing.

- New levels of reliability will be required to obviate, for example, a system malfunction closing down a whole factory. Reliability becomes an even larger problem as greater numbers of less and less sophisticated users are involved.

- Coupled with this is the need for greater security of sensitive data.

All of these factors require progress in software as well as in the systems. Increased processing power can only be achieved through advances in components (microelectronics) and system architecture (the combination of hardware and software systems).

The greatest economic impact of information technology will be at the office and in the factory. That is why these are the chosen fields of application for the ESPRIT program, though no doubt, there will be considerable spin-off for domestic consumer products.

Five areas of research & development have been targeted:

1. Advanced microelectronics
2. Software technologies
3. Advanced information processing
4. Office systems
5. Computer integrated manufacturing

These areas are discussed in the following sections.

Advanced Microelectronics

This area will aim to develop smaller, more reliable and more powerful circuit technology so that devices can perform more functions or operations than those available today. Europe absorbs a fifth of the world's integrated circuit market but produces only 6%. Europe needs a design, manufacturing, and test capacity for very large scale integrated (VLSI) circuits.

The main objective is to provide the technological capability to design, manufacture, and test the very high-speed and very large-scale integrated circuits (ICs), that will be needed in the next two decades.

A concurrent objective is to stimulate R&D on novel materials and devices for special applications. The activities to be pursued include:

- computer-aided design, manufacture and test for very large-scale integrated circuits (VLSIC)

- silicon IC process steps to 1-micron feature size

- integration of process steps, leading toward computer-controlled VLSIC fabrication

- process steps for submicron feature sizes in silicon and other semiconductor materials

- techniques for interfacing ICs to their environment

- research into optical information processing and transmission, notably integrated optoelectronics, optical switching and storage

- novel information and image presentation display

technologies

- novel organic and inorganic materials for electronics and optical technologies

Specific R&D programs in the area of advanced microelectronics are presented in Table I.

Software Technologies

Software technology aims at providing the sound engineering practices, the methods and tools that are needed in the software development process, the management principles for information technology as well as the scientific knowledge underlying them, and aims to integrate them into a consistent technology. It is founded on mathematics, economics, and traditional engineering practices.

A combination of three complementary research approaches will be addressed. The first approach stresses the scientific foundations and covers such areas as formal mathematical techniques, taxonomy and metrics, including empirical techniques and modelling. This approach to software development aims at a better scientific understanding and is predominantly theoretical research work.

The second approach focusses on the software production process. It considers software development as an industrial activity in which large groups of (professional and specialized) software engineers create complex software systems, supported in operation -- in many versions and variants -- for large markets and over a long period of time. Work in this area relates to all parts of the software life cycle and addresses activities like requirements analysis, specification, design, implementation, verification and validation, maintenance and enhancement; of particular importance will be the full integration of methods and tools and the phase-to-phase continuity. Main R&D activity in this area concentrates on methods and tools and their integration into complete systems for software production. The aim is the mastery of the technical production process of software goods.

The third approach is concerned with the software development process as an economic activity in its own right. It focusses on software as a product, investigating the mutual dependencies between commercial goals of an enterprise and the technical characteristics and performance requirements of the software product. It addresses also the problem of producing application-specific software, and the way in which the knowledge about the application domain may influence the tools and methods for software development.

The aim of this approach is to provide the techniques and criteria for organizing, managing, and optimizing all parts of software application engineering and production process. This entails R&D in:

TABLE I
ESPRIT OBJECTIVES: ADVANCED MICROELECTRONICS

SUBMICRON MOS/CMOS

- 0,7 um feature size or better
- 1 million component/chip
- 1 ns delay/gate
- 50 femto-joule/gate

SUBMICRON BIPOLAR

- 0,7 um feature size or better
- 20-50 Kgate/chip
- 50 ps delay/gate
- 50 femto-joule/gate

CAD

- High level CAD system for submicron VLSI
- 10 million components/system
- User friendly
- Libraries of primitive and complex cells
- Use of AIP and expert systems

COMPOUND SEMICONDUCTOR MATERIALS and Integrated Circuits

- GaAs and GaAs/GaAlAs
- 16 Kgate/chip
- 50 psec delay/gate
- 0,3 um minimum feature size

OPTOELECTRONICS

- Components for very high bit rate transmission (2 Gbit/s)
- Wave length multiplexing components
- Integrated electronic and optical components

- theories and methods for program development,
- methods and tools in software engineering,
- economic and industrial software production.

Specific R&D programs in the area of software technology are presented in Table II.

Advanced Information Processing (AIP)

This area will uncover new kinds of direct communications between man and machine -- such as speech and pictures -- with functions that will resemble such human thought processes as assocation and inference rather than just calculation and storage of information.

The objective is to set the basis of industrial exploitation of the transition from data processing to knowledge-processing systems that is the key to the next computer generation. Important objectives on this road include the provision of more user-friendly interfaces to nonexpert users, and the exploitation of VLSIC for a major increase in information processing power.

The main thrust of R&D will be in the following areas:

- information and knowledge engineering, including expert systems
- pattern-recognition techniques and their application to inferfaces with the environment, particularly intercommunication between human and machine
- information and knowledge storage, including novel hardware technologies and advanced software techniques
- computer architecture, particularly for parallel processing, leading to novel processing machines of advanced capability
- design objectives and methods, of embedding trustworthy AIP concepts into VLSIC

Specific R&D programs in the area of AIP are presented in Table III.

Office Systems

Aspects of intelligent interactions between man and machine such as integrated image test speech communication, document creation and distribution will be researched. Machine translation is of particular importance.

TABLE II
ESPRIT OBJECTIVES: SOFTWARE TECHNOLOGY

METHODS, FORMALISMS, AND TOOLS

- Improved methods for systems construction

  - requirements engineering
  - manufacturing approaches
  - product metrics
  - expert system approaches

MANAGEMENT AND INDUSTRIAL ASPECTS

- Incorporate technology advances into the industrial process

- Improve techniques for:

  - quality control
  - reliability control
  - cost control

  for information systems development and production

ENVIRONMENT

- Common infrastructure for

  - general tools
  - services

- Development of

  - interfaces
  - portable tools

TABLE III
ESPRIT OBJECTIVES: ADVANCED INFORMATION PROCESSING

KNOWLEDGE ENGINEERING (KE)

- Development of tools and techniques for the practice of KE
- Construction of demonstrator KBS applications
- Construction of inference demonstrator

INFORMATION AND KNOWLEDGE STORAGE MANAGEMENT

- Investigation of new ways to store and process data, knowledge, meta knowledge through:

  - Quasi natural query language
  - Hierarchical structures for distributed KB
  - Model for manipulation of complex objects
  - Medium and long term research on storage media

EXTERNAL INTERFACES

- Real-time, 2-D image processors
- Design of cursive script recognizer
- Demonstrator of speech recognizer
- First version of picture synthesis processor

COMPUTER ARCHITECTURES

- Multiprocessor machines (prototype)
- Highly parallel architecture (prototype)
- Data flow machines (test of demonstration)
- Reduction machines (demonstrator)
- Inference machines (experimental)
- Connection machines

The objective is to carry out systems research on the information systems that will support the wide range of nonroutine tasks performed by humans in the office environment. The activities to be pursued include:

- office system science, as prerequisite and support to the structural and functional analysis and description of office procedures, definition of standards and the design of adapted office products and systems

- office workstations, document description languages, document creation, and distribution man/machine interfaces

- office communication systems including local area networks and their interconnection, integrated interactive text-voice-image-video communication and value-added functions

- office filing and retrieval systems with emphasis on ease of access to and retrieval of "knowledge," content- and structure-addressable databases, office document languages

- human factors, encompassing all aspects of the interactions between man and information-handling systems

Specific R&D programs in the area of software technology are presented in Table IV.

Computer Integrated Manufacturing (CIM)

Research for factory automation use will relate to the architecture of integrated systems, robotics, sensors, and transducers. This will need further developments in microelectronics and software.

The objective is to establish the technology-base for progressive introduction of computer aids in all phases of the manufacturing process leading ultimately to integrated manufacturing.

The main emphasis is placed on manufacturing elements as they are needed for discrete batch manufacturing, as this is technologically the most demanding problem.

The main thrust of the R&D will concentrate on:

- integrated system architecture for CIM systems, including database management systems and incorporation of AIP (advanced information processing) concepts

- computer-aided design and engineering (CAD and CAE)

TABLE IV
ESPRIT OBJECTIVES: OFFICE SYSTEMS

OFFICE SYSTEMS SCIENCE AND HUMAN FACTORS

- Information analyses of office environments
- Design objectives of office information systems
- Ergonomics of IT equipment and software
- Human factors laboratories

ADVANCED WORKSTATIONS

- Vision, speech, paper, tactile interfaces
- Structured and natural language interfaces
- Office user-support functions
- Architectures of open multimedia workstations

COMMUNICATIONS SYSTEMS

- High-speed network technology
- Standards for interfaces and interfacing
- Multivendor equipments
- Local and wide area network architectures
- Multimedia distributed system network services

ADVANCED FILING AND RETRIEVAL SYSTEMS

- Hierarchies of storage media
- Content addressing of multimedia documents
- Design distributed storage systems
- Effective user-file interface

INTEGRATED OFFICE SYSTEMS

- Architecture and evaluations of comprehensive office systems
- Test environments for office systems
- Application evaluation to feed back to technology design

systems of modular structure

- modular computer-aided manufacture, test and repair systems, and their integration with CAD, CAE
- software and operating systems, including command languages for generation of control programs (starting from design, production, or test simulation data) for automated assembly, for robot operations, or for computer numerically controlled, machine tools
- imaging and control systems for the real-time capture and processing of 3-D images and for generating appropriate responses, incorporating AIP techniques
- VLSIC design and fabrication for CIM subsystems, sensors, etc.
- demonstration models of CIM subsystems leading to complete CIM demonstrators. for experiments in real life situations

Specific R&D programs in the area of CIM are presented in Table V.

Manpower Resources

The overall workplan breakdown of resources for each subprogram is subject to modification in the light of further technological evolution. The partitioning of ESPRIT into five areas is a management convenience and is not intrinsic to the nature of the work. All subprograms are very heavily interrelated.

The resulting approximate total distribution of effort to be supported for the next five years is as follows:

Microelectronics	2140 man-years
Software Technology	1970 man-years
Advanced Information Processing	2070 man-years
Office Systems	1700 man-years
Computer-Integrated Manufacturing	1100 man-years

TABLE V
ESPRIT OBJECTIVES:
COMPUTER-INTEGRATED MANUFACTURING

INTEGRATED SYSTEMS ARCHITECTURES

- Define reference model for CIM systems; and develop support systems where necessary

CAD/CAE

- Develop necessary tools and subsystems for integrated CAD/CAE activity

CAM

- Develop prototype systems for integrated factory operations

MACHINE CONTROL

- Develop prototype systems for machining, joining, and assembly
- Systems and methods for their integration
- Develop methods for optimizing quality and availability

SUBSYSTEMS AND COMPONENTS

- Develop selected subsystems and components; at present these include advanced sensor systems, and microelectronic subsystems for machine control

CIM SYSTEMS APPLICATIONS

- Establish centers of excellence for CIM developments
- Develop selected CIM support applications
    - Product design for automated manufacture
    - Economic models
    - CIM interaction with MIS

13

The Alvey Program for Advanced Information Technology

The Alvey Program is based on the report of the Alvey Committee, "A Program for Advanced Information Technology." The committee's remit was to advise on the scope for collaborative research in IT in the light of increasing overseas competition highlighted by the Japanese Fifth Generation Computer Program.

The Alvey Committee reported in September 1982 and recommended a five year program costing 350 million British Pounds Sterling and involving collaboration between industry, academy and the three government departments involved, the Department of Trade and Industry (DTI), the Ministry of Defense (MoD), and the Department of Education and Science (DES) acting through the Science and Engineering Research Council (SERC). After consultation with industry and other interested bodies, the Government announced its acceptance of the main recommendations of the report and allocated 200 million British Pounds Sterling for the Program, on the assumption that the remaining 150 million would be found by industry. The Alvey Directorate was set up to manage the Program under Brian Oakley who took up his post on June 1, 1983. A small Steering Committee was set up to oversee the work of the Directorate and Sir Robert Telford was appointed as Chairman.

Although the Alvey Directorate is located formally in the Department of Trade and Industry, it is, like the rest of the Alvey Program, a collaborative effort. Its staff are drawn approximately equally from the four main contributors, DTI, MoD, SERC and industry, with industry paying the salaries of the employees seconded to the Directorate. The varied backgrounds of the staff and the fact that they are distributed over a number of locations make it a novel organization and is another way in which the Alvey Program is breaking new ground.

The Directorate came into being in June 1983 but most of the staff did not begin work until later in the year. Seven directors were appointed with responsibilities for specific parts of the Program and for liaison with the three government departments involved. This determined the overall structure of the Directorate.

Alvey has a number of novel features of which the cooperative element is only one. Alvey differs from most other government support for R&D, and certainly that administered by DTI or SERC because it is not primarily responsive but is a directed program. This means that there is a definite strategy with which projects must be consistent and the Directorate is also concerned to establish the cooperative teams that are best fitted to implement the strategy. The strategy is not produced in a vacuum but is the result of extensive consultation and discussion with interested parties in industry as well as in academy. Inevitably some topics that are deserving have to be omitted, whether because of lack of funds, lack of sufficient skills in the UK, or because of the unlikely possibility that the UK would exploit the results sufficiently. The development of the strategies is an attempt to build up within the UK a genuine consensus about what needs to be done. This will be a continuing process and the strategies will be reviewed and updated every year.

The work is being carried out in consortium of firms, academic teams, and research establishments. Practice has shown that the average consortium consists of four or more organizations, typically two or three firms and one or two universities. Some consortia contain more partners, though except for work of a standards type a consortia with many partners would become unmanageable. In virtually every consortium there are universities involved. In addition, there are a number of academic projects of a long range or highly speculative nature, on which it would be unreasonable to expect industry to be carrying out work at this stage in the development. It is required of such academic projects to have someone from industry who will take an interest in the work, steering it towards issues of industrial interest when appropriate, and warning the Directorate when industrial participation should be sought. These are known as "uncle" projects.

Clubs are being established in all parts of the program in order to bring together and act as an information exchange for those in the UK IT community with a direct interest in the field. In general, participants in consortia will be expected to keep the appropriate Club informed of the nature of their work, and the progress being achieved.

Over 300 proposals have been received by the Directorate, and technical approval has been given to about 60 full industrial projects, and 40 academic "uncle" projects. There are over 50 companies in these approved projects, 43 academic bodies, and 5 Research Establishments. Much of the academic work is concentrated in a few centers of excellence where multi-disciplinary teams from different departments in those universities can be brought together to work on the Alvey projects.

The first year of the Alvey Program involved establishing the Directorate and Defining the Work to be done and the means to do it. The initial task was to define the strategies in more detail than had been possible in the Alvey Report itself and to update them where necessary. At the same time, the community needed to be aware of how Alvey was going to operate so that it could start to prepare proposals and could react to suggestions from the Directorate. This was a major exercise and all Alvey Directors have made a point of accepting as many invitations as possible to give talks about Alvey.

Intelligent Knowledge Based Systems

The strategy document describing the IKBS program was published in August 1983 and circulated widely to industry and academy. In anticipation of approval of the Alvey Program, a joint SERC-DoI Working Party was set up in December 1982 under the Chairmanship of Dr. John Taylor of MoD. Between then and May 1983, a number of workshops involving some 40 industrialists and academics were held and wider surveys carried out. The findings were recorded in a three-volume report entitled "Intelligent Knowledge Based Systems -- A Program for Action in the UK." This document was accepted by the Alvey Steering Committee in September 1983 as an interim statement of strategy for IKBS within the Alvey Program.

The Alvey Directorate has asked SERC, and SERC in turn has agreed, to accept particular responsibility for management of the IKBS Program. Of the four "enabling technologies," IKBS is the one that has begun to emerge most recently from academics to a position of industrial importance and therefore, it is appropriate for SERC to have particular involvement in this part of the Alvey Program.

The proposed Program consists of three constituent parts:

- Research Themes and Demonstrators
- Support Infrastructure
- Awareness, Education and Marketing.

Over the past year, the work has developed under these three headings as planned in the report, with the exception of a few significant changes described below.

Under the Research Themes and Demonstrators heading, nine individual Research Themes were listed in the report:

- Parallel Architecture
- Declarative Languages
- Intelligent Knowledge Based Systems
- Expert Systems
- Intelligent Front Ends
- Inference
- Natural Language
- Image Interpretation
- Intelligent Computer Aided Instruction.

The first three Research Themes as listed are being handled together, being equivalent in many respects to a self-contained research program towards fifth generation computing systems. This program under its title of "Declarative Systems Architectures" is concentrating on the support of a limited number of new architectures for parallel computing and intelligent knowledge bases.

The remaining six Research Themes have each had appointed Theme Coordinators charged with the task of promoting the formation of research communities around each of these topics. Most areas have two Coordinators, one from industry and one from academics, with the Coordinators devoting perhaps one day per week to this activity. A principal method of encouraging the formation of these research communities is by organizing specialist Workshops each lasting few days.

Research proposals numbering some 80 in total have been received spread across the areas covered by all nine of the Research Themes. Those approved for support are listed by title in Annex C. Of particular note is the increasing industrial interest in Expert Systems, the entry point for many companies wishing to become involved in IKBS techniques.

The number of proposals for IKBS Demonstrators received has been fewer than anticipated in the strategy document. A major reason for this is the prominence of IKBS techniques within proposals received for Large Demonstrator Projects. For example, of the four Large Demonstrator Projects which have been approved, three have major IKBS content. Nevertheless, proposals for three IKBS Demonstrators have been received, one of which has been approved and two are currently under consideration by the Directorate.

The strategy report calls for the establishment of a common infrastructure of hardware and software which would enable distributed teams to work collectively on projects using telecommunications networks and shared computing facilities. To this end and in collaboration with the Alvey/Software Engineering Directorate, procurement of a number of multi-user mini-computers has taken place. For the IKBS Infrastructure Program, a total of seven GEC Series 63 machines and four Systime 8750 machines (based on VAX 11/750 processor boards) have been installed in research centers, mainly universities. Four other machines have been installed for Software Engineering work. UNIX has been adopted as a common operating system. The machines are being networked together via Alveynet.

Of even greater importance is the standardization of AI language. PROLOG, POPLOG and LISP will all be supported, but every effort will be made to limit the number of dialects of these to be used within the Alvey program. Single user workstations with fast PROLOG and LISP processors will be featured later in the program and studies have been commissioned to assist the Alvey/IKBS Directorate in determining whether development work in this area should be supported.

The IKBS Awareness Program has various facets. A survey of the use of Expert Systems in UK Business has been conducted and reported in a document circulated with Alvey News. Eleven one-hour lectures on IKBS topics by noted UK authorities, mainly from the academic sector, have been video-taped before invited audiences. These are available from the Open University (address: Learning Materials Service, Center for Continuing Educations, Open University, P. O. Box 188, Milton Keynes MK3

6HW). S one-hour videotape showing Expert Systems in action in UK industry has also been planned.

A number of "Community Clubs" are being launched. The first of these, in real-time process control will consist of some 20-30 industrial companies as members, each contributing between 5,000 and 10,000 British Pounds Sterling which will be matched by the Alvey Directorate pound-for-pound. The funds so produced will be used to commission the development by a suitable contractor or contractors of an Expert System, the chosen application being the improvement of quality control in an ethyoxalates plant of Imperial Chemical Industries. A second "Club" in the use of Expert Systems in quantity surveying in the building industry is about to be launched in collaboration with the Royal Institution of Chartered Surveyors. This will look at the use of IKBS techniques in the estimation of costs for major office buildings. Other "Clubs" are under discussion in banking, insurance, accounting, production planning, vehicle scheduling and personnel management.

An Expert Systems "Starter Pack" is being prepared for the Alvey Directorate by the National Computing Center consisting probably of written material, videotapes of Expert Systems in operation and a small number of simple Expert Systems "Shells." The objective is to introduce new users to the technology and take them to the stage where they can move on to the more complex Expert Systems "Shells" now available commercially.

The IKBS Journeyman Scheme is about to be launched to enable industry to send a limited number of staff for six-month periods for hands-on training in IKBS techniques at established centers of excellence in the UK. This staff, on return to their own companies, could help train additional staff, possibly using distance learning material in IKBS when this becomes available. It is hoped that the two centers will be accepting Journeyman from January 1985.

A list of approved projects in the IKBS area is given in Table I. The projects fall into two broad categories, those associated with research and development towards improved IKBS tools (such as improved IKBS software environments), and those which will be based on the use of existing tools in new areas of application of IKBS techniques. A major restraint on the number of proposals in IKBS received, and their size, is the national shortage of staff with experience in Artificial Intelligence and allied subjects.

The Future

The principal challenge of the next few years in the field of IKBS is undoubtedly the creation of a larger pool of manpower skilled in this area. A number of specialist MSc Courses in IKBS in universities have been started and these will produce in their early years between 25 and 50 graduates per year. The requirement of industry and commerce will exceed such figures by a considerable margin because of the growing interest in the applications of Artificial Intelligence in general and Expert Systems in particular. This interest is already strong in much of the engineering industry. There are also signs that use of such techniques in the business world will grow with some activity already apparent in banking, insurance and commodity broking.

The solution of the manpower shortage problem will require a number of approaches in addition to the traditional one of reliance on universities and polytechnics to produce trained graduates. Developments in information technology are progressing so rapidly that continuing education programs are urgently required to keep existing graduates already employed in industry up-to-date in their specialty. Distance learning techniques provide a most appropriate medium and attention is being focused in both the Software Engineering and IKBS parts of the Alvey Program in this direction. Extension of existing universities' MSc courses in these subjects, in collaboration with the Open University, are being examined with a view to provide video-tapes and written material which could be used in a distance learning mode by UK companies for collective in-house training of groups of staff.

Another important approach is learning by practical experience. The pattern has already developed in IKBS applications to the Alvey Directorate that within a typical consortium, one group with considerable experience in IKBS techniques will be found together with a number of other groups at the learning stage. Usually the latter are companies that have been newly elected to apply IKBS techniques in their particular area of industry or business. Such an arrangement makes optimum use of the IKBS skills currently available in the UK and offers the potential of increasing this skill-base by involvement of new personnel in actual IKBS research projects.

The promotion of manpower, training initiatives will prove to be central to the successful expansion in the use of IKBS techniques in UK industry. While it is not primarily the responsibility of the Alvey Directorate to provide financial support for such educational initiatives, the crucial importance of the subject to the future health of IKBS research in the UK does mean that working within its given remit, the Alvey Directorate is doing whatever it can to encourage activities to increase the manpower-flow.

Collaboration

Over the first year of the program grant applications have been received from consortia which involve most of the groups in the UK with prior experience in IKBS and Artificial Intelligence.

Almost all such groups, both industrial and academic, have had grants approved, in some cases as many as three or four.

Thus, with virtually all of the IKBS expertise in the UK already involved in Alvey projects (and some in ESPRIT pilot projects), companies who now wish to submit collaborative proposals are finding it impossible in many cases to involve groups or individual researchers with prior IKBS experience. Some proposals received are from consortia which recognize this difficulty and have taken the only course open to them; that of submitting proposals involving groups with the potential to learn IKBS techniques quickly during the course of the research. Such proposals are not easy to assess but are receiving special attention.

The universities, in which the bulk of the IKBS expertise is vested, in the UK have cooperated fully in mounting collaborative projects with industry. Indeed the pressure on them to expand the size of their groups as fast as they are able has been considerable. This has produced special problems in providing accommodation and facilities for the new staff; the lack of any earmarked funding from the University Grants Committee or other sources for departments called upon to expand in this way is a bar to rapid expansion which should receive particular attention in the appropriate quarter.

Man-Machine Interface

The first priority of the Alvey MMI Directorate, after the appointment of the MMI Director in August 1983, was to formulate the Alvey MMI Strategy. The original Alvey Committee report had focused attention on the sub-topics of Pattern Analysis Displays and the Human Interface. Alvey MMI is a diverse field and each of these sub-topics requires specialist skills. Two separate committees of experts were formed to cover Pattern Analysis, Displays, and the third area of the Human Interface was covered by an Advisory Board made up of experts in this sub-topic, together with the Chairmen of the tow Committees. The responsibility of the Advisory Board was to prepare the Strategy for the Human Interface and to incorporate the contributions of the other two committees in the final document.

The starting point for the Human Interface part of the strategy was a SERC document "The Alvey Program -- A Proposed MMI Strategy" prepared by a team of experts drawn from the universities and industry under the chairmanship of Professor Brian Shackel. Since there was no such precursor in either of the other two sub-topics, the team started from scratch. As the result of an intensive effort, Professor Julian Ullman produced a Strategy for Image Processing. This was developed further by the Pattern Analysis Committee, chaired by Ullman. So far the ideas in these two documents had been generated by a small number of people. It was felt that if the resulting strategy was to be acceptable to the community, their views must also be sought and the two documents were given a wider distribution. Over one hundred replies were received and the final version was subject to further consultation with a large number of the major UK IT companies. General approval was obtained and the strategy was published in the August issue of the Alvey News.

The strategy document is an overview. A parallel activity was therefore started in January 1984 to flesh out the sub-topics and make possible Announcements of Opportunity. This work was done by four Workshops held on Speech Technology, Image Processing, User Interface Design and Design Methods, and Human Factors. The first two have been used for Announcements of Opportunity in Speech and Image Processing. Announcements of Opportunity in the Human Interface will appear in the December issue of the Alvey News. During the development of the MMI Strategy a number of unsolicited proposals were received and they were compared to the emerging Strategy and a number have been approved.

The Committee structure, which was appropriate during the Strategy forming period, is now being modified and links are being made to the DTI Electronics and Aviation Requirements Board (EARB). One of the four Committees reporting to the EARB, the former Control Engineering and Instrumentation Committee, has been reconstituted with a wider brief under the new name Applied Electronics Committee (AEC). This Committee will act as a focus for discussion on the Human Interface and Pattern Analysis aspects of the Alvey MMI Program. Displays fall naturally into the remit of the Advanced Devices and Materials Committee (ADMC). Realizing, however, that all four Committees under the EARB have an interest in Human Interface research, a further ad hoc Committee is being formed which will have members drawn from all four Committees. This committee will meet about twice a year under the Chairmanship of a member of the EARB.

The Alvey MMI/EARB connection will give a high level, industrial input to running the program. It will act in an advisory capacity and eliminate the need for the old MMI Advisory Board. This board will revert to a technical Committee for the Human Interface equivalent to that for Pattern Analysis. A subset of members of each of these two Committees advise the MMI Directorate on the evaluation of projects, namely the Human Interface Proposal Appraisal Advisory Committee (HIPAAC) and the Image Processing Proposal Appraisal Advisory Committee (IPPAAC). Both these Committees make use of independent referees when it is felt that it is necessary to draw on extra technical expertise. The appraisal of speech proposals is made by the Alvey MMI team in close consultation with the Joint Speech Research Unit (JSRU) at GCHQ Cheltenham. Again, referees are used when it is felt that further expert opinion is needed. Display proposals will be appraised in association with LA Division of DTI.

The latest figures are shown in Table I. This commitment represents a total of 21% of the MMI budget. By the end of this

TABLE I
PROJECT OF THE ALVEY PROGRAM

INTELLIGENT KNOWLEDGE-BASED SYSTEMS

- Study for the design of PROLOG machine
- IKBS system architecture based on control flow
- Natural language front end to databases: Project definition study
- IKBS architecture study
- Enhancements to the PROLOG expert system development environment
- Dictionary and morphological analyser for English language process systems
- A model framework for the specification of information systems
- Natural language generation from plans
- Experimental investigation of computational approach to text processing
- Applications of functional closures
- Spatio-temporal processing and optical flow for computer vision
- Extraction of 3-D structure in low level vision by maximising invariance
- Application of IKBS to software project management
- Project proposal for large demonstrator/IKBS design product
- Towards an intelligent help file finder
- Knowledge based systems in hydrology -- A starter project
- Programmer for group research on automatic natural language processing
- A knowledge engineer's assistant for constructing knowledge based fault diagnosis systems
- A computational grammar of English

TABLE I (cont'd)

- Read and write Japanese without knowing it
- Spill Strathclyde project to implement the logic of liquids
- Tools for development of logic programs
- 3-D surface reconstructions and 3-D model innovation from stereoscopic cues (Consortium II of 3D IKBS-vision image interpretation theme)
- Fifth Generation computer architecture
- A parsing tool for the natural language theme
- A knowledge based scheduling system for offshore work
- An information machine incorporating an associative triple store
- An investigation into inference with restricted quantification and taxonomic representation
- A flexible toolkit for building expert systems
- IKBS applications in simulation and avionic tactical decision aids
- Logic based front-ends for large software systems with reference to widely used statistical systems -- GLIM
- IKBS application for mechanical health monitoring
- Application of expert systems for quantity surveying
- An investigation of knowledge acquisition techniques

VERY LARGE-SCALE INTEGRATION

- Enhanced rate RIE
- Dry etching for VLSI
- Plasma processing technology
- Gas phase investigation
- Theory of ion interactions

TABLE I (cont'd)

- Plasma diagnostics
- Gas phase kinetics
- 3rd Generation RIE system
- Ion surface interactions
- Implant and diffusion
- Impurity and defects
- Analytical techniques
- Electron tunnelling
- Two dimensional model
- Model evaluation
- Interactive model
- 2 and 3rd device model
- Direct write study
- E-beam resists
- Microlithography
- E-beam lithography
- Variable shaped E-beam
- Chrome mark etching
- Critical mask measurement
- SEM failure analysis
- Reliability of VLSI
- CMOS-SOS
- Bulk CMOS process
- UHS bipolar
- CDI bipolar process

TABLE I (cont'd

- Bulk CMOS
- Multilevel metal
- Dynamic recoil mixing
- Si MBE for device fabrication
- MBE for silicon VLSI
- Silicon on insulator

VLSI ARCHITECTURES

- Theoretical and empirical models in VLSI computational complexity theory
- Development of a parallel processor chip
- Development of a new parallel computer architecture with dynamic reconfiguration
- Hardware support for software designed as finite state machine
- The script chip project
- Feasibility study for a transputer node
- Investigation into VLSI architectures for computer image generation

CAD FOR VLSI

- Medium term enhancements
- Behavioural languages for VLSI
- Development of working tools for self-test
- Evaluation of INMOS VLSI design system
- Development of a structured CAD system based on advanced bipolar technology
- Concurrent testability design
- Complete CAD system for CMOS VLSI

TABLE I (cont'd)

- Advanced interconnect technology exploitation

SOFTWARE ENGINEERING

- Mechanical verification of applicative systems
- Computing facilities
- Pascal preparation system
- Behavioural description language
- Software fault tolerance in real time systems
- Programming calculus
- IFIP WG2.1 travel
- Graphical kernel system specification
- Reliability and integrity of distribution systems
- ASPECT, multi language IPSE distributed host, distributed target
- Development of VDM toolset
- Workshop in theoretical aspects of specification
- Test specification and quality management
- Promotion of OU course
- Formal requirements specification research
- Categorical programming
- Advanced support environments study
- User workstations and processor bank
- Graphics for requirements analysis
- Use of functional programming as a design and prototyping methodology for intelligent business systems
- Ponder under UNIX

TABLE I (cont'd)

- Automatic programming generation
- ECLIPSE, 1st Generation IPSE for real time and commercial DP
- Algebraic theory of abstract data types
- Theorem proving
- Development of ML
- Formal methods for hardware verification

MAN-MACHINE INTERFACE

- Intonation in computer generated dialogue
- Feedback strategies for N-tuple pattern classifiers
- Voice operated database enquiry system
- Command, control and multiple industrial applications
- Specification, implementation and evaluation of interface systems
- Adaptive intelligent dialogues
- Object identification from 2-D images
- Speech interfacing and phonetic algorithms

LARGE-SCALE DEMONSTRATORS

- Design to product
- DHSS demonstrator
- Speech input wordprocessor and workstation
- Mobile information systems

financial year it is expected that the first three years' funds for MMI will be readily committed. An example of a typical large consortium is the British Telecom proposal for a "Voice Operated Database Inquiry System." This involves BTRL, Logica together with the University of Manchester Institute of Science and Technology and Cambridge University. The aim of this project is to design central equipment which may be called up by the inquirer over the public switched telephone network. It is intended that this equipment will have sufficient built-in intelligence to allow a meaningful dialogue to take place between the caller and the machine to obtain the information required. The project includes a demonstration of these techniques for train timetable inquiries. The research principally involves the design of a suitable dialogue and improvements of the speech recognition and synthesis for it to be used via ordinary telephone handsets and the restricted bandwidth (300 Hertz to 3.4 Hertz) of the UK telephone network.

The coverage of proposals received as a result of the Announcement of Opportunity in speech technology is almost complete, speech coding being the only significant area not covered. The unsolicited Image Processing proposals received do not yet cover all aspects of the Strategy but, it is hoped that further proposals stimulated by the Announcement of Opportunity in the August issue of Alvey News will close the gaps. At this time, there are sixteen unsolicited proposals under discussion in the sub-topic of Human Interface. There are still gaps in the program yet to be covered. The proposals stimulated by Announcements of Opportunity in this area should enable coverage of the majority of fields by the end of this financial year.

The Alvey large scale demonstrator projects are important to the MMI program for two reasons. First, the human interface to them is likely to form an important part of the judgement as to their success -- it is not sufficient that they are just technological successes; they need to be demonstrably usable. Second, the demonstrator projects provide very good vehicles for carrying out MMI research, as they will be early examples of advanced man-machine systems working in environments where the human interaction problems are not yet fully understood or appreciated. Close links have been established with all the demonstrator projects to ensure that the best human interface experience is available, and to identify further opportunities for MMI research within the framework of the demonstrators.

As stated in the Strategy, it is important to increase the awareness of the importance of good user interface design in the design of products. This is not an easy task and very often needs a change of attitude to a more user centered approach. Some equipment suppliers and designers need to be made aware of a user centered design in which the requirements of the end users are identified early in the project development cycle. This requires a knowledge of the users and an analysis of the abilities and needs. The design process has to take a balanced view of these facts together with the technological possibilities. The Alvey MMI program has been devised to provide tools and techniques to help design more effective and usable interfaces. This is the province of the awareness program.

During the past year, most of the larger IT companies in the United Kingdom have formed Human Interface research groups which will act as focal points for advice on Higher Interface matters. The MMI Directorate will try to help them grow and prosper by whatever means available. The first positive steps have been taken in this direction by making sure that top priority is given to collaborative proposals.

The concept of the R&D Technical Centers, outlined in the Strategy, was created so smaller companies could benefit from the Alvey initiative. These Technical Centers are able to offer state-of-the-art services to these companies and help them improve the usability of their products. The centers will also contribute to the awareness of the possibilities for improvement by demonstrating the results of their own research program, and may give encouragement to their client companies to enter into joint research projects with the centers. The first of these centers will come into existence during 1985.

Although the concept of collaboration on R&D in the sub-topics of MMI is new to industrial organizations and universities, there have been no detectable problems presented in the formation of proposals for the Alvey MMI program. Indeed, many of the companies new to the field have seen this as an opportunity to limit investments and risk by forming consortia. The aims of the Alvey initiative to exploit academic research is well exemplified in this area. Most of the research experience lies within academies. Universities with particular strengths in human interface have had no difficulty in finding industrial partners. Good human interface research requires multidisciplinary teams. The Alvey initiative has been able to encourage the formation of teams containing such varying specialist skills as cognitive psychology, computer science, and hardware design. The military establishments have considerable strengths in human interface research. One problem which remains to be solved is how to tap this body of knowledge for commercial exploitation. The work is not of a classified nature very often, but because of the existing commitments, it is sometimes difficult to enter into commercially based consortia.

Small companies are being encouraged to submit proposals. The majority of those that have been able to take advantage of this opportunity have not been able to afford a research department for the life of the project. Other specialist companies have become partners in consortia with the large IT companies which give them other considerable advantages. Out of 34 industrial companies whose proposals are now under consideration, 20 are small to medium sized.

VLSI and CAD

An outline strategy for the VLSI and CAD program was described in the Alvey Report. Further refinement of the strategy from an industrial viewpoint was undertaken by a working group chaired by Mr. B. L. H. Wilson. Other valued inputs have been provided to the directorate. The strategy document was issued in November 1983 and published in the December 1983 issue of Alvey News. This document still provides the program framework.

The VLSI technology program is concerned exclusively with silicon. Any dilution of funding to cover other approaches, notably gallium arsenide, would prejudice the chance of success in what is undoubtedly the key technology for future IT products. However, the rapid evolution of technology means that this is a situation which must be kept under continual review.

The objective of the technology program is to ensure that by the late 1980s the UK has secure access to internationally competitive VLSI. The workplan includes the assembly of selected bipolar and CMOS processes linked to a range of required layer processing techniques. This differs from the approach in ESPRIT, where the whole process and required layer processing steps are contained within a single project. However, the Alvey approach gives rise to the maximum degree of collaboration, in that the program must be viewed as a whole and total success depends on the success of both the layer processing and whole process projects.

The target for the whole process research is "1 micron" technology ready for transfer to production by 1989, with an intermediate target of "1.5 micron" within 2 years. The technology to be developed must be competitive in custom and semi-custom applications incorporating random logic, associated memory, analogue functions, and include improved manufacturability and control over failure mechanisms to permit the design and exploitation of increasingly complex circuits. Fourteen layer processing topics are linked to the whole process work, covering dry etching; ion implantation, diffusion and annealing; multilayer interconnect; silicon on insulator; process modelling; device modelling; microlithography; analytical tools and techniques; silicon material; mask making; packaging and chip interconnect; testing and inspection; reliability and failure analysis; and automated manufacturing. Within each area, a Topic Coordination has agreed to help define a coherent plan and project strategy.

CAD is recognized as being crucial to the exploitation of VLSI circuits. The essential aim of the program is not only to develop the required tools, but also to structure the projects to maximize the availability of integrated tool sets to user companies. The CAD program must be strongly linked in its objectives and timescales with the VLSI technology program. The workplan has four key elements and a degree of cross-linking between them is essential. These elements are:

a. complete integrated CAD systems
b. enhancements to existing systems and tools
c. long-term research into CAD techniques
d. CAD infrastructure.

In recognition of the rapid change in CAD techniques and requirements, there are two phases for deliverables, lasting 2 years and 5 years.

Within the first phase, any development of integrated systems will need to build substantially on existing CAD systems, but in Phase 2 the resulting system will be highly portable, and support a range of technologies and design styles in modular fashion. Although Phase 2 will essentially need to follow Phase 1 as far as the major effort is concerned, it is planned to initiate pilot projects for the definition of Phase 2 projects in parallel with Phase 1. This will allow the optimum system to be selected for Phase 2, although it should not be assumed at this stage that the successful Phase 1 pilot project collaborators will necessarily take on the Phase 2 work within exactly the same organizations. The Phase 2 work will undoubtedly require a major part of the available UK effort in this area and it is hoped that all necessary expertise will be made available to develop the chosen system.

Alongside projects on whole CAD systems, individual research projects on tools and techniques are intended. The objective is to produce tools which will be of wide benefit. Many of these projects will be strongly linked to the whole CAD system project. There is then a strong parallel with the layer processing and whole process aspects in the VLSI area. However, it is probable that the full project structure in this sense will not be in place until Phase 2 of the program. Many of the tools and techniques will need to be tested and employed through enhancement of existing CAD systems.

The VLSI and CAD strategy document recognizes that advanced information processing will require a high degree of parallel processing. The algorithms must be matched to the VLSI circuit architectures if full advantage is to be taken of the advances in technology. Important topics include distributed array processing, systolic arrays and cellular logic with associated research on testability, fault tolerance, redundancy, design complexity, programmability, etc. These areas will not meet all requirements for parallel processing, particularly those arising in the IKBS area.

The current status of the VLSI program is that 35 projects have been approved, totalling 64 million British Pounds Sterling. These projects were announced by the Rt. Hon Kenneth Baker, MP, then Minister for Information Technology, at a Press Conference held on 9 August 1984 and are listed in Table I. These projects provide good coverage of the first 9 topics described above.

Most of the layer processing projects have been approved initially for 3 years on the grounds that the results will be required in that timeframe if the whole process projects are to be successful. Beyond the three year period, the projects are expected to concentrate increasingly on sub-micron techniques or alternative approaches. While the appropriate projects represent a 65% commitment of the total funds, the 3-year approval timeframe implies a much higher commitment of funds in the early years of the program.

The approved projects bring together expertise in the semiconductor industry, universities, Government, and other research organizations. Semiconductor equipment manufacturers are involved in order to advance the UK infrastructure through strong collaboration with device manufacturers. This is particularly the case in the dry etching and high resolution lithography areas. In total, 15 companies are involved with 24 universities and polytechnics and a further 4 research establishments. Full details of the approved projects are given in Table I.

The university involvement is stronger than originally expected and is able to provide specialized knowledge in materials, devices and analytical techniques. They are involved in 23 of the 35 projects, and all but 5 of these projects are fully collaborative with industry.

At present, eight projects have been approved in the CAD area. Four of these are in the techniques research area, addressing behavioral languages, self-test, concurrent testability, and exploitation of advanced interconnect technology. Two others are programs of research to enhance the collaborators, existing CAD systems, and another is a cooperative workstation evaluation project. In addition, one phase 1 whole CAD system project has been approved and another project is planned to be launched within a month or so.

Several gaps remain in the VLSI program, particularly in silicon materials, packaging and interconnect, testing, reliability and failure analysis and computer aided manufacture. However, strategy definition in these areas is now well-advanced and project implementation should be possible in the very near future. A new program on wafer-scale integration has been defined and the first proposals are now under consideration.

In the CAD area, phase 1 projects for whole CAD systems will be announced within a few weeks and pilot projects for phase 2 systems are at an advanced planning stage. The creation of cell libraries for use by industry and universities is considered an important issue. A short-term study on the exploitation and exchangeability of cells is to be launched in conjunction with the MOD VHPIC Application Demonstrator Program. The objective is to examine some key problems in planning the library content and distribution. The results of this study should allow decisions to be taken on implementation of an appropriate program early in 1985.

Information sharing is a central feature of the Alvey program and clubs are to be established as foci for information exchange between participants. In the VLSI and CAD area, a number of research consortia already exist and cover the majority of topics to be researched. In order to avoid duplication of the roles of these consortia and the Alvey Clubs, it is proposed that a single organization formed. Although details have yet to be finalized, it is intended to retain the 3-tier structure of the existing consortia in the Alvey Clubs, namely working groups, main clubs and a committee of club chairmen which would form the Alvey VLSI/CAD Management Committee.

Gallium arsenide material, compound semiconductor circuit technology and optoelectronics are included in the existing consortia but are currently outside the Alvey workplan. However, in order to maintain an overview of the total solid state technology scene, the Chairmen of these consortia will be invited to join the Management Committee.

It is important to recognize that the Alvey program is only part of the research effort within the UK and information sharing would be of benefit in the wider community. For this reason, membership of the Clubs will not necessarily be restricted to Alvey funded organizations. As with the existing consortia, the prime criteria is the ability and willingness of participants to contribute to the information exchange.

The development of the Software Engineering Strategy drew extensively on the considerable work undertaken by a joint Logica/RAL team which was commissioned in the summer of 1982 to prepare papers for consideration by the original Alvey Committee. In the course of that exercise, some 400 people and organizations were contacted and a number of study papers commissioned. Substantial agreement was obtained on the main points to be pursued.

An early activity of the Software Engineering Directorate in the late summer of 1983 was the review of this material and a number of informal discussions were held with key organizations that had made contributions the previous year. As a result, a number of small changes were made, primarily of emphasis, but an overall high level of consensus was reached concerning the main thrusts of the program. At this time, the Computing and Communications Committee (CCC) of the Electronics and Avionics Requirements Board agreed to act as the principal review body and advise the Directorate on the software engineering program. The CCC also expanded its membership to provide added strength to its specialist Software Engineering interests together with an appropriate cross link to SERC's Information Engineering Committee (IEC).

Since publication in December 1983, some 7,000 copies of the Strategy Overview document -- the Software Engineering "manifesto" -- have been distributed, along with 500 copies of the more detailed first version of the overall workplan for those likely to be professionally interested in a specific involvement with one or more Alvey Software Engineering projects. This initial version of the strategy also promised more detailed refinement of the work proposed as the program developed and to date specific sub-strategies have been published in the following topic areas:

Formal Methods -- June 84

Reliability and Metrics -- June 84

IKBS techniques in SE -- August 84

It has been a deliberate policy to expose the Software Engineering program to the widest possible audience likely to be interested in the subject. Thus, in addition to the extensive distribution of the documents noted above, the Alvey Software Engineering team have also taken the opportunity to present the strategy to a wide variety of interest groups with a total audience of more than 1,000 people. All comments received so far have been supportive of the strategy, although sometimes with reservations on emphasis or more detailed definition. Subsequent refinements have gone some way to providing a clearer sense of direction in a number of key topic areas and there will be further developments as appropriate.

A counter to inappropriate bias is the presence of the advisory bodies. As previously mentioned, the CCC acts as the main strategy advisory group primarily concerned with the direction and overall balance of the program. This committee also advises on the funding of research programs in the software engineering area in Government establishments and is well placed to take a national view of activity in this area and thus ensure that high levels of coordination are achieved. To further aid this coordination, links have also been established with SERC's Computing and Communications Committee and SERC's IEC reviews the program on an annual basis with Professor Jones of Manchester University acting as a "link" member between IEC and CCC of EARB.

In achieving the more detailed definition of the program in the important areas of Formal Methods, Reliability and Metrics and Knowledge Based techniques applied to Software Engineering, the Directorate has special advisory groups to accomplish this task:

The Formal Methods Panel -- chairman Mr. Mel Jackson of STC

The Center for Software Reliability -- chairman Mr. Norman Harris of BAe

The IKBS Advisory Panel -- chaired by Dr. Jim Howe and Mr. Tony Dignan, member of the Software Engineering team

In addition to the preparation of the detailed strategy documents in these specialist topic areas, the panels advise on progress and direction; provide advice on work undertaken outside the UK; act as the management nucleus for special interest group activities, and provide a pool of expert referees to offer advice to the Directorate on proposed projects.

The strategy document published in December 1983 identified the following activities as priorities for the first year of the program:

1. The selection of a number of candidate 1st Generation Integrated Project Support Environments (IPSEs) together with supporting tool sets. The aim was to establish a base for demonstrating the effectiveness of the best available current technology in the "Exploitation" section of the strategy and to provide a "bottom up" approach to the provision of 2nd Generation Systems through the incremental improvement of the selected 1st Generation projects.

2. The specific definition of the research lines to be followed in the specific topic areas have been mentioned previously, together with a more complete definition of work to be undertaken in the management process area. This activity to be accompanied by the establishment of an initial portfolio of projects to support the "Innovation" element of the program.

3. To complement the 1st Generation IPSE by undertaking some preparatory requirements work in support of the "top down" approach to the construction of a 2nd Generation IPSE. The 2nd Generation work would commence in earnest in the second full year of the program and would be a major deliverable from the "Integration" element of the strategy.

4. The establishment of an appropriate infrastructure to support the workshop, conference and community building activities that would be reoccurring features of the "Exploitation" element of the strategy and in addition to secure appropriate links with other complementary activities taking place outside the Alvey program.

The pursuit of these priorities has involved the setting up of Alvey Software Engineering projects, the commissioning of direct consultancy activity and specific work by the Software Engineering team.

Before reporting on each of these activities, it is useful to understand that the policy of the Software Engineering team has been to encourage early contact with the Directorate by those setting out to submit proposals. The program is essentially a collaborative one and the construction of a significant collaborative proposal is a non-trivial task. Early contact reduces the chance of significant amounts of nugatory work being carried out, helps both sides clarify the main thrusts of the proposal and usually results in proposals making a better fit with the strategy. Thus, at any point in time, the Directorate has a "pipeline" of proposals ranging from these "formally" submitted to proposals at an early stage of informal discussion.

At the time of writing, some 73 "formal" project applications had been received. 30 have been approved; 23 rejected; 5 transferred for consideration by other parts of the Alvey Program and 15 are currently under consideration. In addition, some 10 further projects are the subject of "informal" discussion with the Directorate and the majority of these are expected to be turned into "formal" applications shortly. Overall, excluding costs for existing SERC STI projects, "infrastructure" and support items, the program now has 25% of its budget committed and would expect to have 35% - 40% committed by the end of the year.

Two of the projects are large 1st Generation IPSE projects -- ASPECT led by SDL and ECLIPSE led by SSL. In selecting these two projects, the Directorate deliberately set out to establish a match with strategy that was both competitive and complementary. Both exhibit state-of-the-art technology and both should be excellent vehicles for incremental improvements towards the goals set for 2nd Generation Systems. In both projects the interests of Real Time system developers are covered in a number of important areas, and in the ECLIPSE project the early stages of the commercial/DP type developer are supported. Essentially, however, the base support environments need to establish that they can accommodate a range of methodologies in the same way that they are expected to support a range of languages.

The examination of requirements for advanced support environments will be an important input to the program for the 2nd Generation IPSE work. A collaborative project has been established to carry out this work. It is intended that the output from this will be public so that the widest possible view of the requirements for such an environment is obtained.

A portfolio of projects in the areas that have been the subject of more detailed definition is now being built up. Of initial interest is:

- the VDM tool set and Formal Requirement Specification projects in the area of Formal Methods.

- the Use of Functional Programming as a Design and Prototyping Methodology for Business Systems in the IKBS techniques area.

- Test Specification and Quality Management in the Reliability and Metrics area.

In addition to these Alvey projects, the Software Engineering Program has taken over the current portfolio of SERC's Software Technology Initiative (STI) projects. All of theses are squarely in line with the main research thrusts of Alvey, and a high proportion of these are in the Formal Methods area.

To assist in securing the infrastructure needed for the efficient running of the Software Engineering program, consultants have been commissioned to undertake the following tasks:

1. Information Service -- The basic requirements for such a service have been established together with an outline set of implementation options. Although the initial requirements have been quite sharply defined, it is clear that the provision of such a service will only be cost effective if it is integrated into a wider Alvey Service.

2. Management Systems -- A basic set of systems and procedures has been defined to enable the Directorate to manage both the program overall and the individual project elements.

3. Technical infrastructure -- The Software Engineering team has actively contributed to the development of the Alvey technical infrastructure policy, taking account of the established SERC Common Base Policy in the Universities and recognizing that a policy for industry needs to place more emphasis on the need for standards in software than on hardware. An early investment was made at the beginning of the year, with IKBS, in additional multi user mini hardware to support a number of selected University centers.

The Software Engineering team also recognized at an early stage that considerable advantage could be gained by establishing good levels of synergy between Alvey and a number of other excellent initiatives that had already been put in place to assist the Software Industry and those working within it. To that end, good working contacts have now been established with:

- The NEDO/DTI Software Tools for Application to Real Time Systems (STARTS): The STARTS software guide, produced by the initiative, represents an excellent survey of the current state-of-the-art within the area and the availability of tools to UK software producers. A member of the Software Engineering team has been invited to sit on the Executive Committee of the Public Purchasers group. This group examines practical ways in which greater levels of professionalism, in both software production and purchase, can be encouraged.

- The Software Products Scheme: In appropriate cases, the scheme can potentially help create a "seamless pipe" that will allow for the support of the development of "idea of prototype" in Alvey and for "product to market" under the SPS. The latest guidelines emphasize the aim of increased synergy between the SPS and Alvey Software Engineering. Good inter-office communications have been established and regular exchanges have been agreed upon with the SPS Advisory Committee.

- The BCS: The BCS's wide ranging interests in the Software field, and the wide membership drawn from software "practitioner," offers the Directorate an excellent potential means of communication with a considerable body of informed opinion. A BCS Software Engineering Task Force has been formed to provide a focus for activity between Alvey and BCS.

Much of the work has been done to define the strategy to be pursued, establishing suitable links with other key programs, setting up an infrastructure to support the work to be carried out, and building up an initial portfolio of projects. By the end of the year it is expected that this initial set of projects will have committed approximately 40% of the budget.

In looking ahead, a number of near term activities are clearly defined:

The strategy will be defined further in respect of a number of key areas:

1. 2nd Generation IPSE -- This will involve a major set of interrelated projects and the 2nd Generation work has been identified in the initial version of the strategy as a major deliverable from the program. It will aim to secure a prototype set of integrated tools and techniques that will be competitive with the best that can be found. Thus UK software producers in the IT industry will have access to UK technology of world class in the latter part of this decade and in the early 1990s and vendors will have world class products.

2. Quality Center -- The strategy asserts that software quality will become increasingly critical to both the supplier and the purchaser and that certification will become an increasing feature of life in the industry. The basic technology to address some of the many issues associated with quality will be addressed, in particular, in the Formal Methods and Reliability and Metrics areas and also in a number of specific toolsets aimed at improving the production and quality processes. More work will need to be directed to this topic and practical ways of making this technology accessible and attractive to both suppliers and purchasers will need to be defined.

3. Management -- The strategy identified that the Software

Engineering Program was concerned with all aspects and roles associated with the software life cycle. In particular, improved techniques, tools, and levels of understanding need to be established so that the software process is better described, modelled and controlled. The lack of response by the industry to this topic clearly indicats the need to spell out more clearly the key issues that must be addressed.

4. The strategy document overall -- The first version of the document undertook to not only develop the ideas set out in more detail in a number of selected areas, but to also regularly review, update and re-issue the document.

In addition to the above strategy issues, it is clear that strenuous efforts will need to be made to increase the project portfolios in the topic areas that have been the subject of further definition in the course of the year.

It is expected that some initial output from 1st Generation projects will take place at the back end of the second year of the program and an important activity will be the development of evaluation projects in conjunction with a number of "definitive users." The range and type of trial user will need to be expanded and consideration given on how the best results of such trials can be disseminated and the community at large encouraged to invest in higher levels of professionalism and more tools. Overall a major activity for the future is the development of more positive links between Alvey, which is fundamentally directed towards "the industry," and the "users" who both use the products of the industry and, in turn, are responsible for approximately of 70% of the Nation's software activity. To assist in this activity the Directorate has commissioned the NCC to set up a User Panel.

The academic community in the UK has developed a well deserved reputation in the field and a number of groups have established a name for world class work, particularly in some of the more theoretical areas. The setting up of SERC's STI in 1982 was designed to strengthen the established groups and encourage the emergence of particular centers of reputation in some of the more practical aspects of Software Engineering. The current active STI projects have been assimilated into the Alvey portfolio, as mentioned previously.

On the industrial side, UK has a significant indigenous hardware industry. As with the USA, the mature hardware manufacturers are also large suppliers of tools with a tradition of R&D in this area. For the newer entrants, this is less clear but is likely to be a requirement for their continued growth and development. Part of the manufacturing industry is associated with the large "system suppliers" i.e., groups not concerned with the specific trade in software but who are vitally concerned with software as an essential component of a traded system. Such companies are also concerned with R&D in the area, but essentially to improve their own internal performance, rather than with a desire to become large scale tool vendors.

The independent software houses in the UK, like their counterparts in other countries, are characterized by rapid growth, their small scale and, their large numbers. They are still concerned with the provision of a service rather than a standard product, with a few exceptions concerned principally with satisfying the UK market need. Experience in Alvey has indicated that R&D, in the techniques and tools area, is patchy -- some actively pursue a clear and deliberate policy of investment, some aim to do so, then trade circumstances, and become sufficiently favorable, and are primarily occupied with maximizing short term revenue.

The industrial funding has principally been tipped towards this latter group but as the program progresses it is inevitable that the hardware and systems manufacturer will take a significant share. What is clear, however, is that the UK's industrial competitors are investing in this area in a major fashion. This represents a clear challenge to the industry to positively identify the opportunities offered by Alvey to increase the effective rate of current investment; to enter new areas, and to take a first step toward becoming acquainted with the subject.

It is still rather early to be clear about how well collaboration is working, but the program has involved ten different industrial organizations, one Government Establishment and nine different universities in full collaborative projects. Eleven university projects are of the "uncle" type with five different companies acting as "uncles." Within the industrial group, a wide range of organizations is represented, from the very small to the very large. At this stage the overall balance of funding currently lies with the software houses rather than the "manufacturers."

It appears that once common interests are identified there is little difficulty in establishing a collaboration between a university and an industrial partner. Software houses, however, show some lack of enthusiasm for co-operation with each other but are ready to work with a manufacturer or user. The larger manufacturers and system companies had, to some extent, started to establish an attitude of co-operation prior to Alvey and exhibit a clear desire to use Alvey to further develop this form of working. All major projects have established clear management structures and good levels of agreement about directions to be pursued and methods of working have been displayed.

The Large Scale Demonstrator Program

A program of large scale demonstrator projects was initiated with the twin aims of producing exploitation led goals for the research in the first place and of demonstrating the results of

Alvey research in real environments at the end of the program. Proposals were invited from companies which could foresee large new markets being opened by the developments which may be expected during the life of the project. 22 outline proposals were considered and of these 7 were selected to be the subjects of sponsored three month studies.

The study reports were considered by a panel of advisors from relevant government departments, and finally by the whole Alvey Board before the final selection of 4 projects to proceed to implementation was made. The prime criterion was the extent to which the proposed demonstrator set goals for the enabling technologies and would show off the results of that research in a working environment.

The total cost (over five years) of the Large Scale Demonstrator Projects is about 37 million British Pounds Sterling of which some 5.4 million British Pounds Sterling can be considered as extensions of the Enabling Technology Programs. Of this total, 7 million British Pounds Sterling is paid (by SERC) to the university members of the projects (100% funded) together with 2.6 million British Pounds Sterling for enabling technology work. The industrial companies pay 50% of the cost of their work on the projects (10.6 million British Pounds Sterling), and the balance is funded by DTI/MoD (14.2 million British Pounds Sterling). Additionally, some of the teams include Government bodies, such as DHSS, TRRL and NEL, who will fund their own contributions to the projects.

Given the primary aim of the Large Scale Demonstrators to set practical targets for research in the Enabling Technology Areas, a close working relationship between the demonstrators and the individual Research Directors has been encouraged. The research proposals in these areas, both within the project, and as Enabling Technology, have been closely monitored by the Directorate Teams and their Advisory Committees. Where suitable, research proposals have not been received, the Directorate is encouraging the setting up of research consortia to carry out the work.

GEC - Design to Product Project

This project will demonstrate the automation of the total production process, from design through manufacture to maintenance in the field. It represents the next generation of Computer Integrated Manufacturing and will use IKBS techniques throughout to capture and apply the skills of the human operators. It will be applied to a new product being designed by Lucas CAV, although the techniques will be suitable for many different product types. This is a very ambitious project, and addresses an area of the highest importance to British Manufacturing Industry, which, while often recognizing the potential of Computer Aided Design and Robotics, frequently finds them too expensive to justify for the relatively small batch sizes commonly found in industry.

The consortium comprises GEC companies, Lucas CAV (as user), the Universities of Edinburgh, Leeds and Loughborough and the National Engineering Laboratory. The Project Leader is Mr. Rex Tomlinson, of GEC Electrical Projects Ltd. at Rugby. The Artificial Intelligence Department of Edinburgh University will examine ways of using Knowledge-based techniques to produce the Design System which is central to this project. The work will use the experience and interest which led to the creation of the inferential mechanical relationship language, RAPT. The Universities of Leeds and Loughborough will use expertise in the area of geometric modelling, which is essential to describe mechanical structures, and will also work on automatic process planning and machine instruction.

Loughborough University's HUSAT will also be working on Human Factors aspects of the Man Machine Interface within this project and incorporate many of the results of the MMI research program. IKBS techniques are central to this project, forming the basis of the design station and also of major importance to the method of generating manufacturing and maintenance information. In Software Engineering, the use of an Integrated Project Support Environment (IPSE) and formalized system specification languages will aid the more efficient generation of software. The Alvey work on VLSI will provide the high speed parallel processing architectures and assist in the implementation of large capacity databases.

ICL -- DHSS Demonstrator Project

In this project, ICL leads a consortium with Logica, the DHSS as user, and the Universities of London (Imperial College), Lancaster and Surrey. The project leader is Mr. Charlie Portman of ICL at West Gorton, Manchester. The project will evaluate the role of new computing technologies in assisting legislation-based organizations, such as the DHSS, in the formulation, interpretation, and application of complex policies and rules. Detailed investigations and demonstrations of intelligent knowledge-based systems, man-machine interfaces, and software engineering techniques will be undertaken as part of the project. Areas to be covered include the determination of the level of supplementary benefits and mobility allowances for individual claimants. The relationship between legislation, policy, regulation, and codes will be examined, and, in particular, the work involved in formulating, modelling, evaluating, drafting and monitoring such rules.

The problems faced by the DHSS which this project aims to resolve, has been attacked by conventional Data Processing techniques with little success due to the scale, complexity and variability of the task. Therefore, this project is of great importance to the computer industry to offer knowledge-based techniques to tackle the problems of such large systems.

The School of Management and Organizational Science at Lancaster University will build the Insurance Officer knowledge based decision support and Policy Modelling demonstrations. The demonstrator research will expand their experience in the role of interpretation and understanding in decision making. The SPAIT Research Group of Surrey University will generate systems to assist claimants in form filling, progress enquiry and determining their eligibility to claim and have considerable experience with the DHSS. The Surrey MMI Research Unit will work on comparing different ways of accessing databases, conduct taxonomic studies of user models of database front-ends, and consider the role of color in interactive displays. Imperial College, London, will be carrying out research to establish methods to check the consistency of policy and regulation in legislative systems.

Among the Software Engineering tasks will be the evaluation and choice of the most suitable languages, techniques for speedy access to large databases, and formal means of preparing software more efficiently. Further work on IKBS includes methods for knowledge acquisition, representation of rules and the means of using this.

Plessey -- Speech Input Word Processor and Workstation Project

Plessey is leading this consortium associated with Shell (as a user) and the Universities of Edinburgh, London (Imperial College) and Loughborough. The project manager is Mr. Peter Schwarz of Plessey, Caswell. Practical Speech Recognition to the standard required by this project is a most exciting and ambitious target (speaker adaptive recognition of connected speech, with a vocabulary of 5,000 words, at minimal error rates). Competition from Japan and the United States will be intense, but if successful the rewards will be very high. Products derived from this demonstrator will include word processors for office use, and many other application areas are predicted.

The bulk of the speech research will be carried out at Edinburgh University. Three Departments, Electrical Engineering, Linguistics, and Artificial Intelligence will work together on the project and will be managed by the new Center for Speech Technology. Their task will be the generation, in software, of almost the entire speech transcription system, using a large amount of research in Natural Language Understanding and Phonetic Feature Extraction aimed at the understanding of unconstrained speech. Imperial College, London, will undertake the continued development of the ALICE computer architecture, and will research methods and tools to support the development of software using declarative languages and ensure the smooth transition from environments (VAX and XEROX Dandelion computers) being used for speech research to the Alice target hardware. The HUSAT team at Loughborough will be responsible for the Human Factors aspects of the project, undertaking various experiments, investigations and simulations to ensure the optimum development of the user interface (MMI).

This project will demand major advances in capability in all the Enabling Technology areas. The processing power required to recognize speech in real time will require a high degree of complexity and speed on silicon. Advanced 1 um CMOS processes will be used, and Wafer Scale Integration hopefully will become available in the timescale. "Fifth generation" techniques of parallel architectures, content addressable memory, and IKBS will be crucial to achieve a practical working product. If successful, this could make a major impact on world markets, despite heavy international competition.

Racal -- Mobile Information Systems Project

This project concerns the design of a range of highly intelligent, mobile IT terminals that can communicate with various public and private databases via radio links, taking advantage of the new Racal cellular radio service.

The consortium comprises a number of Racal companies, Acorn Computers and the Universities of Cambridge, Loughborough (HUSAT), Surrey, Sussex and the Open University. User organizations within their consortium are BL Technology, the Transport and Road Research Laboratory, the RAC, and the Electricity Council. The project is lead by Dr. John Walker, of Racal Research Ltd. at Reading. The IT techniques that will be employed to provide a number of services to the motorist are:

Route Guidance to plan and guide optimum routes for motorists, saving time, money and frustration.

Traffic Information for up-to-date information on traffic incidents and road conditions.

A Mobile Electronic Office with Portable Terminals to provide a remote mobile terminal for computing, access to databases, wordprocessing, electronic mail, diaries, expert systems, etc.

Mobile IKBS, with access to a wide range of IKBS.

In this Demonstrator, two examples are chosen:

Fault Diagnosis in the Electricity Network
Condenser/Collator for Road Traffic Information

Acorn Computers have considerable experience in volume markets for computer products that will be valuable for this project.

The HUSAT team at Loughborough will investigate the ergonomics of terminals for mobile use and the Human Factors aspects of Mobile Information Systems. The Cambridge University Computer Laboratory will research the design of generalized interfaces, protocols and networks. At Surrey University, the Department of Electrical and Electronic Engineering will work on "Formal Methods," an important new technique in Software Engineering to assist in the efficient preparation of software.

Sussex University will be working on the IKBS for the Traffic Information System (Collection and prioritization of information from police and motoring organizations, etc.) and the formatting of messages and broadcasting strategy. The Open University will be working on the IKBS for fault location in the Electricity Network.

Since this project will lead to a range of mass produced products for use in vehicles, it will be essential to have a range of low cost, high performance custom VLSI chips. Only CMOS will have this performance, matched with the very low power consumption required.

AWSAP Project

A further project is also under consideration, the Advanced Workstation and System Architecture Project (AWSAP). When the Large Scale Demonstrator Program was started, several of the proposals received related to the development of Work Stations for the next-but-one generation. It was soon recognized that such workstations or "work cells" would comprise a series of modules, many of which would be Fifth Generation Computers. These modules would have to be interconnected and work together in a way more analogous to the architecture of existing computers than to the conventional data network. As thinking on future architectures began to crystallize, the need for this supervisory layer of architecture became more apparent. This view was voiced by many delegates to a workshop on Parallel Architectures held at Warwick University in July 1984. A user with a complex task to be performed must be able to rely on the collection of heterogeneous parallel architecture modules working together in a way that is quite transparent to him. Both the hardware and the software of the system must act in an integrated fashion.

Representatives of the companies which made "workstation" proposals to the Large Scale Demonstrator Program met at Churchill College Cambridge for a two-day workshop in December 1983 to examine the possibility of setting up a project to generate the required architecture. The meeting concluded that a fully collaborative project involving staff from all relevant companies would be desirable and could achieve agreeable results. Such a project would require the staff to be co-located and that a three month study would be mounted to act as a prototype for the project organization while establishing the case for the project as a whole and making firm proposals for the organization and promotion of the scheme.

Seven companies (Ferranti, GEC, ICL, Plessey, RAcal, STC and Thorn-EMI) signified their willingness to second members of staff to the study. The team began work in April at the Shoreditch campus of Brunel University, and the report was published in early July. The report proposed a project which would use a team of about 25 staff members over a four year period and cost some 4 million British Pounds Sterling. The resultant architecture would be used by as many firms as possible in the UK and would be considered as the basis for international standardization. The report stressed the fact that the UK IT industry was fragmented and that the individual firms made little or no impact in the world scene. On the other hand, the combined strength of the companies concerned could thus wield considerable influence.

The study proposed that the first year should be spent in the generation of a provisional architecture and at this stage consider opening the project to European participants. This may involve the project becoming an ESPRIT program and could prove to be a useful step on the way to international standardization. The next year and a half would be engaged in developing the detail and simulating and validating the designs as they emerge. The final phase involves the construction of a prototype system based on the system architecture and using prototype product modules developed by the various collaborators to comply with the standard requirements.

The Alvey Directorate is considering the report in conjunction with potential participating companies.

Architecture

Work on architecture appears in various parts of the program. It forms part of the VLSI section, in the form of special circuits, primarily for signal processing which can be used as demonstrations of the VLSI technology. It is a major feature of the IKBS section, with architectures, for parallel inference machines and knowledge base access. It is also a feature of the Image processing part of the MMI section, where special architectures for this purpose will be developed.

It will be possible to support only a very limited number of developments. One of these is likely to be a development of the ALICE architecture from Imperial College where a consortium is forming to carry the development forward. The prototype is likely to be used for the speech input word processor Large Demonstrator. There is a plan to build a simulator on which new architectural ideas can be emulated, if only because of the cost of developing systems in hardware.

Work is in progress to see if a Compiler Target Language can be developed, based primarily on work at Imperial College and Manchester University, to provide a means of buffering parallel language developments from various architecture developments.

The AWSAP project may provide a framework for linking various architecture modules into a system, a supervisory layer.

The Information Technology Training Initiative

Representatives of GEC, Plessey and Racal held discussions to see whether there were any steps that could be taken to reduce the effort and money expended in competitive recruitment of electronic engineers and computer scientists. They concluded that it would be better to attack the root of the problem -- the overall shortage of suitably trained graduates. It was felt that a form of distance learning might be used to both convert graduates who had started life in non-relevant disciplines and to update existing employees as technology develops. Such a process would prove costly in the first instance and a request was made to the Alvey Directorate to act as a catalyst in obtaining more general support for the scheme.

Although the most obvious source of distance learning material is the Open University, there are several others including Aston, which has developed a facility for generating Tutored Video Instruction material, and Heriot Watt, which has built up a large catalogue of American material to which it has access. In addition, many companies have developed isolated lectures and courses, which when brought together, might form a powerful range from which flexible curricula could be built.

Professor John Sparkes of the Open University was commissioned to undertake a 3 month study and make recommendations of the operation of a scheme for the IT industry. The study concluded that a comparatively small team could validate and modify existing material and then commission additional courses where necessary. Sparkes concluded that such an operation would need "pump priming" finance of about 1 million British Pounds Sterling over a two year period, but would then become self sufficient through fee income. The report was presented to a meeting of industrial representatives on 7 June 1984 and there was substantial agreement that some form of initiative is necessary in this area. There was a general feeling that the pump priming finance could be shared by Government and Industry. The role of the Alvey Program is seen as purely catalytic and the Government role would probably be taken over by the Manpower Services Commission in the long run.

An interim management committee has been formed from representatives of Industry, MSC and QE Division of DTI. Robert Neal has been seconded from the British Broadcasting Corporation to undertake the task of establishing the initial curriculum, working with existing industrial programs to establish a number of trial courses and drawing up firm plans for the longer term development of the initiative. At the end of 1984, the committee should have a plan that can be supported fully by the Government and Industry and will lead to full scale operation by the Spring of 1985.

Alvey Computing Infrastructure

Any research program needs tools, and for IT research these tools are principally the computing infrastructure of software, systems and communications. The Alvey program was heir to earlier IT programs run by the SERC and has, over the year, been building on the inherited base of tools through a number of initiatives within the enabling technologies and the Directorate as a whole.

To coordinate the investment by each Alvey technology in computing infrastructure, a working party was set up to produce a policy on standards that could be used throughout the program and a report has been issued as a consultative document. In this report, each Alvey technology sets out a policy on software standards, and proposals are made for the implementation of the policy through a support program. The Directorate sees this coordinated approach to the provision of the basic tools as vitally important in order to maximize collaboration, effectively disseminate research results, and promote their successful exploitation in industry.

Software Engineering and IKBS in Alvey have both taken over and expanded the earlier SERC initiatives. In the case of Software Engineering, this has meant a continuous widespread use of the ICL PERQ which has been supported by the SERC's Common Base Program. The policy has also been extended to multi-user minis with support for software development on the VAX 11/750 and, in collaboration with IKBS, the new GEC Series 63 systems being purchased with Systime 8750 systems being placed at the principal software development sites. Each site has been funded to employ a service manager and development contracts have been placed at the development sites. A team at the SERC's Rutherford Appleton manages and coordinates the project which represents a major investment in supporting a UK product. Both Software Engineering and IKBS have put substantial effort into the evaluation of new personal workstations in collaboration with the SERC Common Base Project. The High Level Hardware Orion system has been selected for new language development work and it is expected that other systems will be selected for general purpose work. To complete the range of resources available, Software Engineering and IKBS are investigating a mainframe service running all the standard software for the computationally intensive projects.

The MMI Directorate expects to concentrate resources on providing single user systems and is evaluating systems with the other categories. MMI research is very closely related to IKBS and the infrastructure policy reflects this in the coordinated approach being taken to the support of tools for both communities.

VLSI and CAD infrastructure policy differs in some respects from the other enabling technologies. For VLSI technology projects, the requirements tend to be specialized and project specific, so general policies are of less relevance. For CAD, the program is dominated by pre-existing industry investment in software and hardware. This is matched by a strong research base in the industrial companies. The main emphasis is on defining CAD interfaces standards to promote portability and sharing of software components.

For all systems supported by the enabling technologies communications will be provided in line with the policy defined by the Infrastructure Director.

14

Computer Aided Manufacturing—International (CAM-I)

Computer Aided Manufacturing-International, Inc. (CAM-I) is a not-for-profit organization. It was formed in 1972 to further the cooperative research and development (R&D) efforts of companies with common interests in computer aided design and manufacturing (CAD/CAM). The corporation is member owned and supported by industrial, governmental and educational organizations in Australia, Europe, Japan, and North and South America.

CAM-I's primary mission is to meet industry's need for long range planning and development of computer system design and prototype software which will increase productivity and improve the quality of working life.

Representatives from CAM-I's member organizations participate in goal-oriented projects and committees. These projects and committees develop and test advanced prototype systems that will increase human capabilities in the manufacturing environment. CAM-I's cooperative development program improves member representatives' understanding of CAD/CAM through the exchange of ideas. Public recognition and acceptance of the use of computers is enhanced through CAM-I's international seminars and library distributions.

CAM-I has 95 Industrial and Governmental Members (Table I) and 52 Educational Members

The activities of CAM-I are coordinated through a full-time professional staff. Research and development plans, including budgets, timetables, task assignments, and measurement criteria, are created by CAM-I project and committee representatives with staff support. Internationally recognized experts in CAD/CAM technology are contracted to perform CAM-I research and development. All contract work is performed under the guidance of the member representatives and the CAM-I staff. Project and committee representatives meet quarterly to contribute ideas, propose concepts, review plans, and make decisions concerning proposed research and development programs. These meetings are held in various regions and are closed to the public except by special approval.

CAM-I holds periodic international technical conferences for members and nonmembers to explore new areas of technology. CAM-I's Annual Meeting each Fall provides a public forum to conduct general business activities, review the status of existing projects and committees, and present new technology. Public seminars, workshops, and training courses on developments of current interest are also sponsored periodically by CAM-I.

The CAM-I library contains proceedings, minutes, reports, proposals, specifications, prototype software, and training

TABLE I

U.S. INDUSTRIAL & GOVERNMENTAL
SPONSORS OF THE CAM-I PROJECT

Air Force Materials Laboratory
Allen-Bradley Company
AMP, Inc.
Applicon MDSI
Arthur D. Little
Avco Aerostructures
Bell Helicopter Textron
Bendix Corporation, Kansas City Div.
Boeing Commercial Airplanes
Boeing Computer Services
Booz, Allen & Hamilton
Catepillar Tractor Company
Cincinnati Milacron Inc.
Computervision Corporation
Control Data Corporation
Cummins Engine Company, Inc.
Deere & Company
Denelcor, Inc.
Digital Equipment Corporation
Douglas Aircraft Company
Dresser Industries
DuPont deNemours, E.I.
Eastman Kodak Company
Emhart Corporation
Evans & Sutherland
General Dynamics/Convair
General Dynamics/Fort Worth
General Electric Company
General Motors Corporation
Gerber Systems Technology
Gould Inc. S.E.L.
Graftek (Graphics Technology Corp.)
Grumman Aerospace Corporation
Grumman Data Systems Corporation
Honeywell, Inc.
Hughes Aircraft Company
Koppers Company, Inc.
Lawrence Livermore Laboratory
Lockheed-California Company
Lockheed-Georgia Company
Lockheed Missile & Space Company, Inc.
McDonnell Aircraft Company
McDonnell Douglas Automation Company
NASA-Ames Research Center
Northrop Corporation
Otis Engineering Corporation

TABLE I (cont'd)

Sandia Laboratories
Sperry Corporation
3M
TRW, Inc.
Union Carbide Corporation
United Technologies Corporation
Westinghouse Electric Corporation

materials, either developed by or donated to CAM-I. Development results, when completed and tested, are dedicated to the public domain, and along with other nonproprietary documents, may be purchased from the library.

Project Overview

CAM-I is currently engaged in seven active Projects and the Electronics Automation Program. The Geometric Modeling Project will provide a means to computerize the access of geometric data from conceptual design to finished product. The Process Planning Program, using this geometric data, is developing a system to capture the logic required for the generation of process plans. The Advanced N/C and Sculptured Surfaces Projects are enhancing the use of computerized tools for controlling these production processes. The Factory Management Project is developing a hierarchical information system to facilitate efficient management of the actual production activities. The Electronics Automation Program was designed to satisfy the special requirements of the electronics industry and has specific short-term projects in component data description, device simulation, data exchange between CAD/CAM systems, testing, and manufacturing control. A new Project approved in 1983 by the board of directors addressing Computer Aided Quality Assurance has begun its program to model an overall structure of computer aided quality assurance as it relates to the various aspects of CAD/CAM and to identifies and develops those areas where the needs for applications of computer technology are most immediate for integration into the overall system. Initially, the project will concentrate on programming methods for coordinate measuring machines. The Robotics Software Project has also received the board of directors approval in 1983. The increased complexity of robot application and their integration into flexible manufacturing systems requires efficient off-line programming and simulation techniques. In the future, programming for robots will utilize sophisticated graphic simulation techniques. The software systems and languages, including graphics and simulation techniques, will be addressed in the Robotics Software Project development program. As well as being cornerstones for the future, these Projects offer concepts for significant improvements in productivity for today's environment.

CAM-I Framework Project

A logical, evolutionary plan is needed by organizations in order to implement computer aided design and manufacturing systems at their own pace. Not only must technical feasibility be considered in such an undertaking, but likewise the economic, social, and organizational framework into which such systems are integrated.

This Project will develop a system framework for the integration of manufacturing functions through computerization. This Project will define the nature of the framework, the boundaries within which applications should be constrained, and the needed interfaces between them.

The main objectives of the Project are to:

- Define a system framework for CAD/CAM that is as independent as possible of present or predicted computer hardware and software.
- Describe an overall CAD/CAM system framework capable of simple orientation to an individual company.
- Provide a means for an easy and efficient replacement or enhancement of individual applications systems.
- Provide boundaries and guidelines for future development activities.

Project highlights include:

1979 - Framework Project was formed for the purpose of analyzing the requirements for integrating various manufacturing functions through computerization

1980 - Donation of ICAM Architecture (ICAM Composite View of Aerospace Manufacturing) by U.S. Air Force provided a manufacturing model for use as a basis for further development.

- CAM-I developed systems were incorporated into the ICAM model to assess boundaries and interfaces
- State-of-the-art hardware and software interfaces were also analyzed in terms of the overall manufacturing model

1981 - Efforts were started to revise the ICAM Architecture into a sequence (network) of activities

- Existing CAD/CAM systems were analyzed to determine generic and unique features of each; and examine the relationship between them and the ICAM Architecture

Geometric Modeling Project

Computers are used increasingly to convey information about the shapes of objects. To convey this information, it is necessary to describe, store, and represent complete data pertaining to complex three dimensional figures. A geometric modeling system filling these requirements is needed to provide the geometric database which can be assessed by other design, manufacturing and testing elements of a true computer integrated manufacturing system.

This Project will develop an advanced three-dimensional geometric modeling system that will allow the flow of geometric and other related information to be fully automated and integrated through the product design and manufacture process.

The main objectives of the Project are to:

- Develop specifications for a generalized geometric modeling system through the stepwise formulation of functional specifications, designs, and prototypes of the various components composing such a system.

- Establish consistent terminology for geometric modeling.

- Evaluate, guide, and disseminate related technology developments.

Project highlights include:

1979 - Boundary Representation contract awarded to McAuto

- Interface Study of COMPAC/CAPSY/CAPP awarded to University of Berlin

1980 - Applications Interface study identifying communications means between applications and geometric modeler begun by Shape Data, Ltd.

- Contract study on PADL-1 modeler completed by New Mexico State University

1981 - Boundary Representation study placed in public domain

- Applications Interface study completed

- TIPS-1 solids modeler documentation translated from Japanese to English by Cornell University

- Project began studying feasibility of integrating the CAM-I Sculptured Surfaces processor with GMP Boundary File

1982 - IBM version of TIPS-1 and accompanying English documentation released to public domain

- RFQ issued on design of a method of representing dimensioning and tolerating data in a geometric modeling system

Process Planning Program

Improved industrial productivity increasingly hinges on the ability to produce quality products inexpensively, satisfy the demand for greater product variety, and introduce more flexibility into product designs. A major portion of these industry needs can be met by automating the process of converting design data and manufacturing knowledge into work instructions for making specific products.

This Project will develop a series of advanced process planning systems capable of increasingly automatic generation of manufacturing process plans and work instructions from product description data.

The main objectives of the Project are to:

- Identify and capture the logic of process planning.
- Specify the necessary part description information and develop required system interfaces.
- Develop evolutionary process planning systems capable of operating in a variant mode (using group technology to modify similar existing plans) and a generative mode (applying planning logic to geometric and other part description data).

Project highlights include:

1977 - CAPP 2.1A software completed

1978 - Automated Time Standards Module delivered

1980 - Process Planning Data Requirements Document published

1981 - CAPP 3.1A, DEC PDP 11/70 minicomputer version offered

1982 - Process Planning Logic and Methods Study completed

- Detail Conceptual Design Model of Experimental Planning System, XPS-1, completed

Advanced N/C Project

Today's numerical control processors require considerable programming time, effort and skills. Furthermore, they are statement-oriented, sequence dependent, and severely limited in terms of economical part production and tool path verification. There is a need for an advanced NC processor which is capable of utilizing bounded geometry representation, alphanumeric input/output, graphics, generative programming, and other characteristics of more advanced computer integrated manufacturing systems.

The Project will develop a fully computerized numerical control processor capable of automatically generating optimum tool paths and automating machine technology decisions.

The main objectives of the Project are to:

- Develop and implement new automated tool path generating techniques, capitalizing on three-dimensional bounded geometry for the part description and identification of material to be removed.
- Create an advanced numerical control (ANC) processor which will interface with other systems (geometric modeling, process planning, etc.) receiving available input and generating required output.
- Expand processor output information and produce NC verification data.
- Improve reliability and accuracy of tool control as compared to current systems.
- Automate the fabrication processes such as tool selection, setup instructions, feeds and speeds, operation sequencing, etc.
- Expand processor applications to other than machining, such as inspection, robotics, and material handling.

Project highlights include:

1977 - Advanced Numerical Control Project was founded to develop a bounded geometry NC processor

1978 - Advanced NC system specifications were prepared by General Dynamics/WDSC and Northern Illinois University

1979 - Advanced NC processor Conceptual Design was completed by General Dynamics/WDSC and accepted by project sponsors

1980 - An 18-month contract for Detailed Design of an Advanced NC system was awarded to McDonnell Douglas Automation (McAuto)

1981 - Contractor, McAuto, began work on detailed design of the Advanced NC processor - to be completed in 1982

Sculptured Surfaces Project

Industry has a need to define and manufacture objects with complex, contoured surfaces. Currently, major problems exist in the mathematical representation and numerical control machining of the difficult, contoured geometry frequently encountered in specific manufacturing applications.

This Project will develop and integrate the required technology to support the definition and manufacture of complex surfaces.

The main objectives of the Project are to:

- Develop a comprehensive set of sculptured surface capabilities using the structure of CAM-I's existing sculptured surfaces processor with its bounded geometry attributes.

- Develop an advanced system to include capabilities not currently available for designing and machining complex sculptured surfaces, including more advanced precision tool design.

- Extend the existing sculptured surfaces hierarchical geometry for compatibility with solid three-dimensional geometric modeling.

- Advance the state-of-the-art in sculptured surfaces technology and make this technology widely available throughout the industry.

Project highlights include:

1975 - Computer Aided Sculptured Pre-APT (CASPA) system released. The processor permits definition of sculptured geometry; determines cutter position for model milling and passes geometry on to APT; and contains complete graphics package.

1976 - SSX5 system incorporating "Surface through General Curves" definition completed by Northern Illinois University (NIU)

- SSX5A and SSX6A systems providing powerful regional milling capabilities completed by NIU

- SSX7 and SSX7A incorporating an improved splining algorithm, three-corner patch capability and improved ARELEM and regional milling capabilities implemented by NIU

1978 - Further improvements in ARELEM and regional milling, and a method of decomposing large surfaces into smaller fragments were main features of SSX8 release by NIU

1980 - Documentation for SSX8 released by NIU

1981 - Messerschmitt-Bolkow-Blohm (MBB) released the SSR1 system which features expansion of translator tables, recompilation of all FORTRAN routines to identify ANSI deviations, implementation of new mathematical and extraction functions, and restructuring of the release tape.

Factory Management Project

Industry continues to encounter problems in meeting near-term manufacturing schedules and balancing shop work loads. This situation is in turn compounded by the fact that about 50% of all work instructions are modified on the shop floor. These conditions highlight the need to develop a flexible factory information system which can monitor, report, control, and efficiently manage a facility's total manufacturing resources.

This Project will seek to model and demonstrate the technology needed for an advanced information system capable of managing factory operations. The key to achieving this is improved data collection/measurement and the development of a closed loop information system which will allow more rapid and accurate communication between work centers and production control functions.

The main objectives of the Project are to:

- Improve data collection, acquisition and measurement.
- Develop distributed database support of individual management levels.
- Identify techniques that will aid in predicting decision results.
- Specify a closed loop communication and control system.

Project highlights include:

1979 - Structured Systems Analysis and Design (SSAD) selected as project modeling technique

- Functional Specifications for an Advanced Factory Management System was condensed and published

1981 - Conceptual Model of Shop Floor Data Collection and Reporting Completed

- Final Report on Factory Data Collection delivered
- State-of-the-art comparison of (283) commercial manufacturing systems was published
- Analysis of the Factory Management System Interface with Resource Planning was conducted

Electronics Automation Program

Electronics CAD/CAM has progressed rapidly in specialized applications. There is a need, however, to tie these applications together into a unified system. To do so requires an ability to exchange data among systems users, suppliers, subcontractors, and others. This implies not only a means of data exchange, but a bank of standard electronic components information to draw from, the ability to simulate design data using a generic modeling language, the capability of automating electronics manufacturing processes, and a system for integrated testing of simple to very complex, multifunctional devices.

This Project seeks to advance the development and application of computer aided design and manufacturing (CAD/CAM) techniques within electronics. The Advanced Planning Group, which involves all electronics Automation sponsors, reviews technical subject areas, conducts evaluations, and establishes new projects of interest to sponsoring companies. Activity within each of the individual projects is aimed at establishing specific requirements, formulating specifications and requests for quotations, monitoring contracts and evaluating deliverables.

Initial projects identified for sponsorship include:

- Electronic Components Data Bank
  Objective: Create the design of a data bank for standard electronic components information and specifications.

- Electronics Simulation
  Objective: Describe components in a generic modeling language that will enable them to be used in electronic simulation processors.

- Data Exchange
  Objective: Design a data exchange interface that will allow various electronic CAD/CAM systems to communicate directly with one another.

- Electronics Manufacturing
  Objective: Develop guidelines and technical specifications as to how additional and advanced manufacturing equipment can be integrated into electronics CAD/CAM.

- Integrated Testing
  Objective: Determine the feasibility of developing a universal data base format and structure that can be accessed by any properly prepared automatic test system.

Project highlights include:

1981 - Electronics Automation Interest Group met in both Europe and U.S. to draft program specifications and long range plan

1982 - Electronics Automation Program achieved project status and formulated specific project objectives. Electronics Project activities proposed include:

Components Data Bank
Electronics Simulation Modeling
Data Exchange
Electronics Manufacturing
Integrated Testing

Robotics Software Project

The incorporation of robots into production factories has increased greatly in recent years. In conjunction with flexible manufacturing systems and CAD/CAM, Robotics is expected to lead revolutions in production systems during the next generation. Benefits from robotic activity are being researched and evaluated against the more traditional production methods.

Robot manufacturers have made considerable advances in hardware development, but software developments have mainly been concerned with the teaching playback method. It has become apparent that the current software technology developments are now beginning to switch from the teaching method to the language method. The increasing need for further development and refinement of robotics hardware and software will effect a greater demand in the near future for increasing numbers of robots, their improved functional capacity and a higher artificial intelligence capability. Potential for a wide variety of standard software interfaces with the development of robot softwares and their standardization is an area that must be explored. While many robot applications will use written language for off-line programming, in the future graphic methods will be an increasing requirement. However, the basic software structure must be developed irrespective of the input language methodology be it written languages, graphics, or completely automated. Consequently, the Project will concentrate on basic developments and drive toward interim standards recommendations.

The Robotics Software Project will investigate all areas of robotics software such as:

- Teaching Playback Software

- Robot Language

  Survey
  Work Language
  Operation Language

Motion Language
Standardization
Processor Development and Evaluation
Postprocessor
Expansibility
Off Line Programming

- Artificial Intelligence

  Visual
  Touch
  Pattern Recognition

- Robot Control

  Optimum Control
  Application Control
  Error Recovery

- Modeling

  Robot
  Environment
  Solid Model

- Simulation

  Computer Graphics
  Interference Checking

- Sensors and Processing Software

- Multiple Robots Cooperative Motion

- System

  Interface with FMS
  Robot Interface Standard
  CAD Robot Interface
  Robot Independent Software

- Management

  Economics
  Safety
  Human Interface

The four major areas of development for this Project are:

1. Clarification of Robot Software System Structure

There are two methods for input of robot instructions: Teaching and Language. The instructions given from these inputs are compiled and sent to the controller system as control information for each mechanical joint of the robots, and these are finally forwarded to the controllers of the robots' physical components.

The third subsystem, the simulator system, is a necessary factor for off line programming, whereby the robot motion in the environment is displayed by the use of a model. The significant subject facing future robotics software development is how the robot independent part can be integrated or programmed into a system to receive input from the various software data sources. Figure 1 which was first proposed by Professor Okino of Hokkaido University, the Interest Group Chairman, and then refined within the Interest Group effort, is indicative of a future practical robot software structure, including the present teaching playback method, on-line inputs by languages, and off-line programming simulation, as well as new concepts such as robot independent teaching system, robot geometric model, machinery/dynamics model, controller model, sensor model, initial robot motion data, and final robot motion data.

2. Study, Study Material Arrangement, In-Depth Research and Discussion of a Practical Proposal for Robot Language Standardization

The second subject of development, robot languages, will be conducted with consideration given to every current and foreseeable function of robotics software and its relation to robot languages, with an eye toward the goal of language standardization. Although a standardized language for robots is a major goal, it is anticipated that many initial developments resulting from the work toward standardization will be of great benefit in the near term.

3. Prototype Robot Software Development Within the Framework of The Three Subsystems

Prototype software development has been selected not only for the direct benefit of actual practical development work, but also in anticipation of the benefits that can be derived from the discussion of general software matters and their relationships to other areas of study.

4. The Study of graphic input techniques for robot programming, investigation of graphic simulation methods, recommendation for progressive development from the basic robotic software Concepts to utilize graphic programming techniques, and the methods of integration into CAD/CAM Systems leading to automatic programming of robots will also be considered.

The CAM-I Robotics Software Interest Group surveyed the practical uses of and the need for industrial robots in the manufacturing processes of industrial companies throughout the world. A detailed survey of existing robots used revealed that most of them were designed for specific work, such as painting, welding, and assembly, and were, for the most part, labor-saving robots

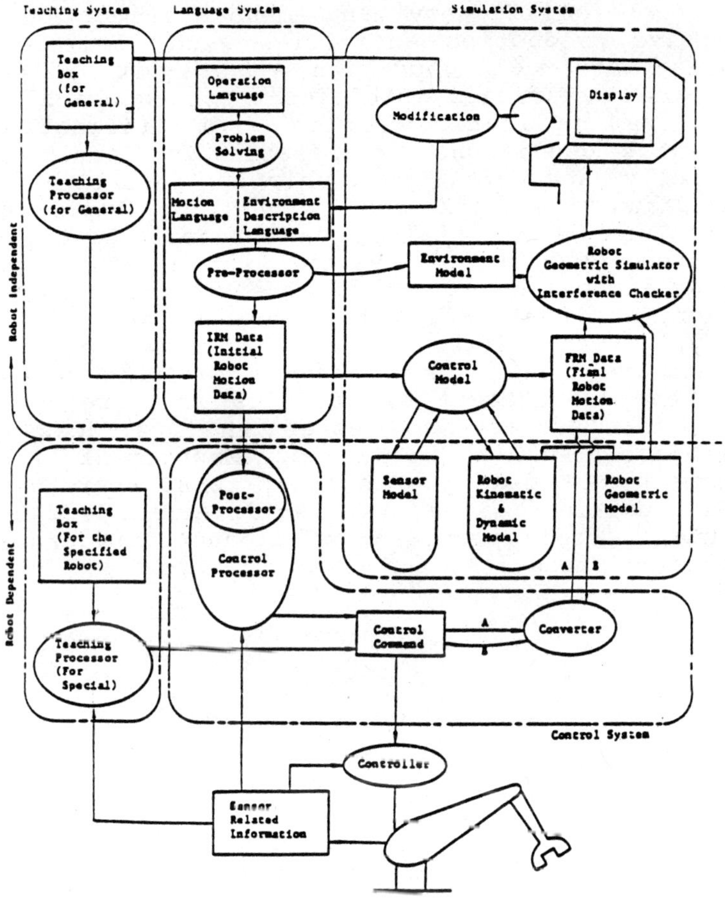

Figure 1. The original concept for the structure of robotic software for the CAM-I project as proposed by Prof. Okino of Hokkaido University.

utilized solely for the performance of non-complex production work. A large number of these robots are gradually being automated for more dedicated applications. There is a growing need today for artificial intelligent robots with the capability of being integrated into other types of production systems, being built into overall factory management systems, and being applied to extensive production activities with flexible manufacturing techniques, etc. In addition, there is a need for more sophisticated artificial intelligent robots which are well suited to extensive application fields from utilization in certain environmental conditions undesirable for human labor, to the substantially accurate, very highly reliable, overloaded or complex structured work that cannot be implemented by human effort. Although initially the project development will be concentrated in robotics system software and languages, there will be an increasing effort directed to graphics input, graphics simulation, and eventually, to automatic programming for robots. The study in these latter areas will proceed in parallel with the basic software system developments. Meeting these common needs requires the enhancement of robotics software. As part of its activity, this Project will establish interfaces with the other CAM-I Projects, such as the Factory Management, Process Planning and Geometric Modeling Projects, and thereby increase the robotics function as a viable integrated CAD/CAM tool to contribute to the improvement of productivity and reliability of manufacturing processes.

15

System Development Foundation (SDF)

The System Development Foundation, a California nonprofit corporation, was organized by the Rand Corporation in 1956. From its inception until 1 July 1969, the Foundation was called the System Development Corporation and conducted itself as a private operating organization qualified under Section 501(c)(3) of the Internal Revenue Code. Its major activity was the performance of contracts for the United States Air Force to meet air defense and other national security needs. It also performed work for other military and nonmilitary agencies of the government and, to a limited extent, for industry.

On 1 July 1969, the original System Development Corporation changed its name to System Development Foundation and transferred all contracts, and substantially all assets and personnel, to a new for-profit organization which took the name System Development Corporation (SDC). In exchange, the foundation received 100% of the new corporation's outstanding stock. The foundation retained the original charter, but changed from an operating organization to a grantmaking organization. The foundation's Board of Trustees then adopted a program to concentrate its grants over the next few years among eligible nonprofit organizations studying the information sciences and human-machine interface.

From 1969 to 1981, the foundation implemented this program by making major grants of SDC stock to California Institute of Technology, the Rand Corporation, Stanford University, and the University of California at Berkeley. Sale of this stock by the recipient institutions supported the following programs:

> California Institute of Technology: Support for the computer science program, primarily founding of the Silicon Structures Project to develop VLSI technology.
>
> Rand Corporation: Support for Rand-sponsored research projects, publications, and educational programs.
>
> Stanford University: Renovation of facilities for the Department of Computer Science.
>
> University of California at Berkeley: Purchase of hardware for the Department of Electrical Engineering and Computer Sciences and creation of a revolving fund to permit prompt exploitation of research opportunities.

In January 1981, when SDC was purchased by Burroughs Corporation, sale of its remaining SDC stock to Burroughs provided the Foundation with the funds to conduct its current grantmaking activities. On 14 December 1981, the foundation's Board of Trustees decided on the fields in which its further grants would be concentrated. This decision was announced in a press release reading as follows:

The System Development Foundation presently seeks to advance the information sciences. The foundation initially will make grants for basic research in the field. Grants will be made for a duration appropriate to the research problem, normally more than one year. The foundation is focusing presently on the following specific research areas:

(a) Principles of information science, including spatial and content information theory, classification, and information structures;

(b) Principles of representation in biological and machine information processing, as exemplified by neurobiology, the cognitive sciences, non-von Neumann computer architectures, and robotics;

(c) Principles underlying the human-machine interface, including engineering and cognitive approaches to human factors in individuals and groups;

(d) The interface between the computer and artistic endeavor.

The following information is from the "Report of the Director of Programs" in the 1983 Annual Report:

Since May 30, 1981, the System Development Foundation has developed and implemented a program to support basic research in the information sciences. By June 30, 1983, the Foundation had approved more than $36 million in grants under this program. The Foundation's program was developed under two constraints. First, it was decided that the Foundation should focus primarily on those areas which the System Development Corporation had initially been created to address: namely, "the information sciences, information processing and the human-machine interface." Second, it was decided that the Foundation should operate for a finite term rather than in perpetuity. Within approximately four years, the foundation expects to make its last grant.

Within these constraints, a program was developed around two strategic principles. The first principle was concentration of force. While not precluding the extraordinary opportunity, the program would focus on a few well-delineated areas with a common goal. The second principle was uniqueness. Because of the small size of the Foundation's assets relative to those of other potential donors, the program would complement, rather than supplement, other funding.

To determine how these principles would apply, a survey was made of the funding by other grantmaking organizations (including the federal government) and of activity in the information sciences. A number of resulting observations helped focus the program. One was that basic research itself is important; it provides the ideas and understanding that are necessary for real progress to take place. Another observation was that the climate for basic research throughout the sciences, and particularly in the information sciences, was surprisingly bad. Researchers could usually find short-term support for research projects with low risk and immediate application. However, they were increasingly unable to find the sustained support necessary to focus on fundamental questions, where the payoff, while potentially very great, was neither immediate nor assured. Further, what support was available was often not sufficiently concentrated to generate a critical research mass.

Within the information sciences, while products were (and are) being developed rapidly, there was little attention to the search for basic principles. Nevertheless, the field included talented scholars who desired to pursue such questions, given financial support. Also, the cost of encouraging outstanding basic research in the information sciences appeared to provide greater potential benefit than other programs in keeping with the foundation's goals and resources. On this basis, in December 1981 the Trustees issued the statement of program and approved the first grants for basic research in the information sciences. The building of the program has been based on the following premises:

* The goal of science is to understand principles; seeking that goal is an efficient way to achieve practical results in the long run.

* Science is a process in which theory is not mere metaphor, but must be predictive and empirically testable; the process is one in which experiments are performed so that their results may be analyzed, incorporated into models, and used ultimately to inform theory.

* There are principles of information science.

* Understanding semantics (of both formal and natural language) may well be the same problem as developing a true information theory.

* The limits of knowability - indeterminancy and uncertainty in all their forms - are a principal means of bounding otherwise unbounded problems: the treatment of these limits is central not only to understanding the nature of information, but also to advancing everyday analysis and computing.

* Constructive methods are perhaps more important and certainly more interesting than existence proofs.

* The foundation would, when necessary, consider supporting institutional process (e.g., technical meetings), as well as specific research.

* The foundation should make gifts only when no other sources are available, when all other sources together are insufficient, or when no other source can be timely enough.

Within the information sciences, specific topics where support for basic research might make a significant difference were selected. The foundation's gifts have so far been directed at eight such topics. The table at the top of page 5 summarizes the total grants approved from 30 May 1981, through 30 June 1983.

The program as a whole can be described as a fundamental investigation into representation, meaning, and cognition. For each topic the nature of the opportunity is somewhat different. All eight categories involve investigation of the principles of information science. In seven of them the investigation is unified around some intermediate focus, such as language. The first category, which is labeled principles of information science, includes those investigations which go directly to the basic thrust of the foundation's program. Applications range from data base construction to the design of integrated circuits. The substrates for computation range from copper and silicon through nerve tissue to DNA and RNA.

Computational linguistics and speech is a field exploding with ideas. For example, viewing the generation, interpretation, and acquisition of language as a computational process provides new constraints for language research. It takes the deus ex machina out of linguistic theory and forces the investigator to explain in empirically verifiable detail how meaning is extracted from surface structure. Similarly, viewing computation as a linguistic process appears to offer important insights into the nature of computation that have direct implications for practical programmers. It now appears that a common flood of ideas, and support in this area has been directed primarily toward the engineering of applied systems rather than an understanding of fundamental principles.

Research in symbolic mathematics seeks to represent mathematics, an already highly formalized body of knowledge, in such a way that computing devices can efficiently use that knowledge in solving real problems. Up to now, symbolic computation has consisted largely of algorithmic assistance for algebraic manipulation. In the past, software engineering problems have held object-oriented programming, however, it is now possible for researchers to identify the real problems of representing and applying mathematics. These problems are particularly important both because of the general import of the subject matter and because the test cases cannot be wriggled away from. It is straightforward to tell if a result is correct, and because of the size of the problems, the solutions must also be efficient.

In robotics, the foundation is supporting studies of the principles of locomotion, manipulation, and perception, rather than ad hoc solutions in these areas. In all three areas the same principles apply to animals as to artificial devices, such as robots. The investigations seek to bring out those common elements. Also, the foundation has helped to strengthen the field by supporting the first robotics journal and sponsoring a small annual conference covering the breadth of robotics.

When the foundation was beginning to develop its program, it quickly became clear that the principles underlying parallel and distributed computing, i.e., <u>non-von Neumann computation</u>, need to be much better understood. Almost all computer development since 1945 has been based on the von Neumann model of a single processor to control execution of instructions and data drawn from the same memory. At present, computer science lacks the concepts and the formal notation to treat computation that goes beyond the von Neumann paradigm. The foundation's early support of work in non-von Neumann computation has provided an important start for an area of study that is rapidly gaining support from other sources.

In the <u>neurosciences</u>, the study of representation and meaning is the investigation of how thinking about the real world takes place on a neural substrate. Machine computation has provided the neurosciences with new theoretical approaches but, much more importantly, with a new ability to test theory. With computer models, researchers can show for the first time precisely what theories of neural activity predict will happen in complex systems of neurons. Thus neuroscientific theory can at last be directly connected with experiment. The foundation has sought to assist the development of such theories and of the analytical tools to connect them to experiments. Research in the neurosciences should provide an important check on the generality of theories of information processing derived from experience in digital computers.

The <u>human-machine interface</u> has several dimensions. There has been outstanding research on the basic physiology of human interaction with computers. During the last two years, there have also been an increasing number of sound psychological and other studies of one-to-one interaction between human beings and computers. The foundation has encouraged the search for basic principles governing this interaction to guide and supplement the large existing efforts to engineer specific solutions. Another area in need of study is the complex and somewhat diffuse interaction of computer systems with human organizations. It has been surprisingly difficult to find qualified researchers with ideas about how to address this interaction.

The foundation has become a principal supporter of <u>computer music</u>, a field in which art and science meet. The grants have been primarily to three universities for a period of five years. It is hoped that these grants will permit them to continue their artistic explorations until their research leads to expressive, inexpensive computer musical instruments. Thus, when these grants expire, large-scale support should no longer be required for computer music research, composition, and performance. The problems of computer music tie directly to the other interests of the foundation. For example, a central problem of the computer musicians is linguistic: to understand enough about the formal structure of musical ideas to represent them expressively and easily to both human beings and machines. Similarly, dimensional analysis suggests that a computational architecture for computer music must be based on a non-von Neumann concept.

It should be noted that the emphasis and balance of the foundation's giving have shifted over time, and will continue to shift. Entire topic areas may be added or deleted. Within all eight topic areas, the foundation has actively sought out potential investigators, in addition to reviewing proposals received. It is often asked by what criteria the foundation evaluates possible research projects. Many considerations come into play; however, a few are always present:

* The importance of the questions being investigated

* The originality of the investigator's approach

* The initiative and intellectual quality of the investigator

* The realism of the investigator's plan

* The appropriateness of the subject area to the foundation

The foundation's program has only begun and is starting to see scientific output and publication from a few grants.

16

How to Keep Up with New Developments

Information on progressive research results is published by each of the 8 major projects. The following sections provide information on obtaining future information on the projects.

ICOT

ICOT has no system for sending ICOT publications automatically. However, a list of publications is available, and individual publications are sent on request. Contact:

Yumiko Okada (Ms.)
International Relations
Institute for New Generation Computer Technology
Mita Kokusai Bldg. 21F
4-28 Mita 1-Chome
Minato-ku, Tokyo 108 Japan
Tel: (03) 456-3195
Telex: ICOT J32964

Information on ICOT developments is published in the journal New Generation Computing, produced by Ohmsha, Ltd. (Japan), and distributed by:

Springer-Verlag
175 5th Avenue
New York, NY 10010
(212) 460-1500

MCC

Information on the Microelectronics and Computer Technology Corporation should be requested through:

William D. Stotesbery
Director, Government and Public Affairs
MCC
9430 Research Blvd.
Echelon Building #1, Suite 200
Austin, TX 78759
(512) 343-0860

SRC

An annual report, including a Chairman's Statement and Executive Director's Statement, is available from:

M. U. Regan, Publications Coordinator
Semiconductor Research Corporation
P. O. Box 12053
Research Triangle Park, NC 27709

DARPA

Information on developments in the Strategic Computing Project may be obtained by writing to:

Dr. Clinton Kelly, Director
DARPA
Strategic Computing Project
1400 Wilson Blvd.
Arlington, VA 22209-2308
(202) 694-3622

ESPRIT

Official documents on the ESPRIT program are published in the Official Journal of the European Communities, available from:

Office for Official Publications
of the European Communities
L-2985 Luxembourg
Tel. 49 00 81

The most useful issue is generally the Draft Council Decision adopting each annual work program, which is published in mid-January.

Alvey Directorate

The Directorate issues an annual report each January which is published by the Institution of Electrical Engineers. A wide range of other Alvey publications is also available from:

Janet Tomlinson, Editor
Alvey News
Institution of Electrical Engineers
Savoy Place
London, WC2R OBL United Kingdom

CAM-I

The form below is provided by CAM-I for information requests.

PLEASE TELL ME MORE ABOUT CAM-I

Name____________________ Title____________

Department____________________ Mail Code____________

Company ____________________ Telephone____________

Street or P.O. Box ____________________

City, State, Zip Code ____________________

☐ Please send me an application for membership.

☐ Send me more information on CAM-I's technical program.

I am especially interested in . . .

_____ Framework Project	_____ Sculptured Surfaces Project
_____ Geometric Modeling Project	_____ Factory Management Project
_____ Process Planning Program	_____ Electronics Automation Program
_____ Advanced N/C Project	_____ Other__________ (specify)

☐ Please send me more information on CAM-I's . . .

_____ Library Services	_____ Meetings and Seminars

☐ Please add my name to receive CAM-I newsletter (bimonthly).

For Office Use Only

☐ Corporate ☐ Meetings & Expos ☐ Other

The completed form may be mailed to:

CAM-I, Inc.
611 Ryan Plaza Dr.
Suite 1107
Arlington, TX 76011

SDF

Information requests on the System Development Foundation should be addressed to:

Charles S. Smith
Director of Programs
System Development Foundation
Suite 210
181 Lytton Avenue
Palo Alto, CA 94301

An annual report is published in June.

17

Directory to the Projects

INSTITUTE FOR NEW GENERATION COMPUTER TECHNOLOGY
Mita Kokusai, Bldg. 21F
4-28 Mita 1-chrome, Minato-ku
Tokyo 108 Japan

Kazuhiro Fuchi
Director

K. Furukawa

K. Murakami

T. Yokoi

K. Kawanobe

T. Kakuta

R. Onai

S. Uchida

R. Nasr

L. M. Pereira

K. Ueda

T. Chikayama

H. Motoda

F. Maruyama

Yumiko Okada (Mrs.), International Relations

MICROELECTRONICS AND COMPUTER TECHNOLOGY CORPORATION
9430 Research Blvd.
Echelon Building #1, Suite 200
Austin, Texas 78759-6509
(512) 343-0860

Officers

Admiral B. R. Inman
Chairman, President, and Chief Executive Officer

Dr. John Pinkston
Vice President and Chief Scientists

Palle Smidt
Senior Vice President, Plans and Programs

R. G. Rutishauser
Vice President, Finance and Administration

George D. Black
Vice President, Human Resources

Program Directors

Dr. Woodrow Bledsoe
Artificial Intelligence/Knowledge Based Systems Program

Dr. Eugene Lowenthal
Data Base Architectures Program

Dr. Peter C. Patton
Parallel Processing Program

Raymond Allard
Human Factors Technology Program

Dr. John Hanne
VLSI/CAD Program

Dr. Barry Whalen
Semiconductor Packaging and Interconnects Program

Board of Directors

Phillip W. Arneson, President, Amphenol
Allied Corporation
Columbia Rd. & Park Ave.
Morristown, NJ 07960

Robert L. Cattoi, Vice President, Corporate Engineering
Rockwell International Corporation
600 Grant St.

Pittsburgh, PA 15219

Robert A. Fuhrman, Group President
Lockheed Missiles and Space Company
255 Hollywood Way
Burbank, CA 91503

Gregory Harrison, Vice President, Corporate Services
National Semiconductor Corporation
2900 Semiconductor Dr.
Santa Clara, CA 95051

William C. Hittinger, Executive Vice President
RCA Corporation
30 Rockefeller Plaza
New York, NY 10020

William G. Howard, Jr., Vice President and Corporate Director
Motorola Corporation
1303 E. Algonquin Rd.
Schaumburg, IL 60196

Admiral B. R. Inman, USN (Retired)
President and Chief Executive Officer, Chairman of the Board
Microelectronics and Computer Technology Corporation

Michael F. Maguire, Senior Vice President, Sector Executive
Harris Corporation
Melbourne, FL 32919

Robert B. Murray, Vice Pres. & Director, Corporate Planning
Eastman Kodak Company
343 State St.
Rochester, NY 14650

Don O. Neddenriep, Group Vice President, Product Division
Sperry Corporation
1290 Ave. of the Americas
New York, NY 10104

Allan M. Norton, Vice President, Technical Operations
Martin Marietta Corporation
6801 Rockledge Dr.
Bethesda, MD 20817

Robert B. Palmer, Executive Vice President,
Semiconductor Operations
Mostek Corporation
1215 West Crosby Rd.
Carrollton, TX 75006

Ryal R. Poppa, Chairman
President and Chief Executive Officer
BMC Industries, Inc.

1100 American National Bank Bldg.
St. Paul, MN 55101

Robert M. Price, President and Chief Operating Officer
Control Data Corporation
8100 34th Ave., S.
Minneapolis, MN 55440

James J. Renier, President, Information Systems and
Vice Chairman of the Board
Honeywell, Inc.
Honeywell Plaza
Minneapolis, MN 55408

F. Grant Saviers, Vice President, Storage Systems Development
Digital Equipment Corporation
9 Riverside Rd.
Weston, MA 02193

George M. Scalise, Senior Vice President,
Chief Administrative Officer
Advanced Micro Devices
901 Thompson Pl.
Sunnyvale, CA 94086

David Simpson, President and Chief Operating Officer
Gould Inc.
10 Gould Center
Rolling Meadows, IL 60008

Thomas T. Tang, Vice President Research & Development
NCR Corporation
1700 S. Patterson Blvd.
Dayton, OH 45479

SEMICONDUCTOR RESEARCH CORPORATION
300 Park Drive, Suite 215
Post Office Box 12053
Research Triangle Park, NC 27709
Telephone: (919) 549-9333

Staff

Larry W. Sumney, President
R. C. Alberts, Staff Vice President, Policy & Planning
R. M. Burger, Ph.D., Staff Vice President, Research
R. K. Cavin III, Ph.D., Director, Design Sciences
W. C. Holton, Ph.D., Director, Microstructure Sciences
R. E. Darby, Jr., Director, Administration
J. J. Cox, Program Manager, Packaging
J. R. Key, Ph.D., Program Manager, Technology Transfer
M. D. Connelly, Manager, Information Systems
S. E. Connor, Administrative Support Assistant
R. D. LaScala, Contract Administrator
S. R. Fallin, Secretary/Word Processor Operator
T. S. Johnson, Secretary/Word Processor Operator
K. A. Olive, Administrative Support Assistant
M. U. Regan, Publications Coordinator
K. A. Spruil, Travel & Conference Coordinator
C. L. Taylor, Financial Assistant
S. D. Thomas, Administrative Services Coordinator
W. M. Wagnor, Finance Administrator

Board of Directors

Mr. Eugene J. Flath (Chairman
Intel Corporation
3065 Bowers Ave.
Santa Clara, CA 95051

Mr. Michael J. Callahan
Monolithic Memories
2170 Mission College Blvd.
Santa Clara, CA 95050

Mr. Jon E. Cornell
Harris Corporation
Melbourne, FL 32919

Mr. Gregory Harrison
National Semiconductor Corporation
2900 Semiconductor Dr.
Santa, Clara, CA 95051

Mr. Bob J. Jenkins
Motorola, Inc.
1303 E. Algonquin Rd.
Schaumburg, IL 60196

Dr. Jeffrey C. Kalb
Digital Equipment Corporation
9 Riverside Rd.
Weston, MA 02193

Mr. Albert C. Kibbler
Honeywell, Inc.
Honeywell Plaza
Minneapolis, MN 55440

Mr. J. W. Lacey
Control Data Corporation
8100 34th Ave., S.
Minneapolis, MN 55440

Dr. Paul R. Low
IBM Corporation
Old Orchard Rd.
Armonk, NY 10504

Mr. Carmelo J. Santoro
Silicon Systems, Inc.
14351 Myford Rd.
Tustin, CA 92680

Mr. George M. Scalise
Advanced Micro Devices, Inc.
901 Thompson Pl.
Sunnyvale, CA 92680

Dr. Fred Schwettman
Hewlett-Packard Company
3000 Hanover St.
Palo Alto, CA 94304

Mr. Tim B. Smith
Texas Instruments, Inc.
P. O. Box 225474
Dallas, TX 75265

Mr. Larry W. Sumney
Semiconductor Research Corporation

Technical Advisory Board

Dr. R. M. Burger (Co-Chairman)
Semiconductor Research Corporation

Dr. James M. Daughton (Co-Chairman)
Honeywell, Incorporated
Honeywell Plaza
Minneapolis, MN 55408

Dr. Grant A. Beske
E. I. Du Pont de Nemours & Co.
1007 Market St.
Wilmington, DE 19898

Dr. Wilmer R. Bottoms
Varian Associates
611 Hansen Way
Palo Alto, CA 94303

Dr. Charles T. Brodnax
E-Systems, Inc.
P. O. Box 226030
Dallas, TX 75266

Mr. Don Butler
General Instrument Corporation
1775 Broadway
New York, NY 10019

Dr. Steve Campbell
Sperry Corporation
1290 Ave. of the Americas
New York, NY 10104

Dr. Bernie Chern
National Science Foundation

Dr. Billy L. Crowder
IBM Corporation
Old Orchard Rd.
Armonk, NY 10504

Mr. Melvin Davis
Goodyear Aerospace
1210 Massillon Rd.
Akron, OH 44315

Dr. Conrad Dell'Oca
LSI Logic Corporation
1601 McCarthy Blvd.
Milpitas, CA 95035

Mr. J. Philip Downing
Advanced Micro Devices, Incorporated
901 Thompson Pl.
Sunnyvale, CA 94086

Mr. Robert F. Elfant
Burroughs Corporation
Burroughs Pl.
Detroit, MI 48232

Mr. R. M. Goldstein

AT&T Bell Laboratories

Dr. Dragan Ilic
Hewlett-Packard Company
3000 Hanover St.
Palo Alto, CA 94304

Dr. S. V. Jaskolski
Eaton Corporation
100 Erieview Plaza
Cleveland, OH 44114

Mr. Gary Kelson
Silicon Systems, Incorporated
14351 Myford Rd.
Tustin, CA 92680

Dr. Harold W. Korb
Monsanto Company
800 N. Lindbergh Blvd.
St. Louis, MO 63166

Dr. W. W. Lindemann
Control Data Corporation
8100 34th Ave., S.
Minneapolis, MN 55440

Mr. Robert D. Lohman
RCA Laboratories
30 Rockefeller Plaza
New York, NY 10020

Dr. Michael Michael
Westinghouse Electric Corporation
Gateway Center Westinghouse Bldg.
Pittsburgh, PA 15222

Dr. Frank Micheletti
Rockwell International
600 Grant St.
Pittsburgh, PA 15219

Dr. Arnold Miller
Xerox Corporation
Stamford, CT 06904

Dr. Gerry Parker
Intel Corporation
3065 Bowers Ave.
Santa, Clara, CA 95051

Dr. Kenneth A. Pickar
General Electric Company
3135 Easton Tpke.

Fairfield, CT 06431

Dr. G. R. Mohan Rao
Texas Instruments, Inc.
P. O. Box 225474
Dallas, TX 75265

Mr. Raymond P. Roberge
Union-Carbide Corporation
Old Ridgebury Rd.
Danbury, CT 06817

Mr. Michael Tynne
Monolithic Memories, Incorporated
2170 Mission College Blvd.
Santa Clara, CA 95050

Dr. Thomas Sanders
Harris Corporation
Melbourne, FL 32919

Mr. L. David Sikes
Motorola, Incorporated
1303 E. Algonquin Rd.
Schaumburg, IL 60196

Dr. Court Skinner
National Semiconductor Corporation
2900 Semiconductor Dr.
Santa Clara, CA 95051

Dr. Kenneth slater
Digital Equipment Corporation
9 Riverside Rd.
Weston, MA 02193

University Advisory Committee

Professor Charles E. Backus
Arizona State University
Tempe, AZ 85287

Professor Stephen W. Director
Carnegie-Mellon University
5000 Forbes Avenue
Pittsburgh, PA 15213

Professor Robert M. Hexter
University of Minnesota
Morris, MN 56267

Professor David A. Hodges
University of California at Berkeley
Berkeley, CA 94720

Professor John G. Linvill
Stanford University
Stanford, CA 94305

Professor Nino A. Masnari
North Carolina State University
Raleigh, NC 27650

Professor Paul Penfield, Jr.
Massachusetts Institute of Technology
Cambridge, MA 02139

Professor Stephen D. Shapiro
State University of New York at Stony Brook
Stony Brook, NY 11794

Dr. Joseph Stach
Massachusetts Technology Park Corporation

Professor Andrew J. Steckl
Rensselaer Polytechnic Institute
Troy, NY 12191

Professor Ben G. Streetman
University of Texas at Austin
Austin, TX 78712

Professor Edward D. Wolf
Cornell University
Ithaca, NY 48103

DEFENSE ADVANCED RESEARCH PROJECTS AGENCY
U. S. Department of Defense
Strategic Computing Project
1400 Wilson Boulevard
Arlington, VA 22209-2308
(202) 694-3622

Robert C. Cooper
Director

Lynn Conway
Assistant Director

Dr. Clinton Kelley
Program Manager

Steve Squires
Computer Architecture

Paul Losleben
Program Manager Infrastructure

ESPRIT
European Strategic Program for Research and Development
In Information Technology
200, Rue de la Loi
B-1049 Brussels, Belgium
Telephone: 235-4477 or 235-3859
Telex: 25 946 JEPE B

E. Davigon
Vice President, Commission of European Communities

John Hawgood
Advisor, University of Durham

Walter Heimann
Advisory Board, Siemans

Malcom Pelty
Advisor

Alvey Directorate
Millbank Tower
Millbank
London SW1P4QU U.K.

Mr. Brian Oakley
Executive Director

Mr. D. L. A. Barber

Mr. M. Buck

Dr. R. Crispin

Dr. W. Fawcett

Dr. D. Hartley

Mr. M. Newman

Mr. D. Talbot

Mr. D. B. Thomas

Dr. T. Walker

Dr. R. Witty

Steering Committee

Mr. P. Hughes
Logica Holdings Ltd.

Mr. J. Leighfield
ISTEL

Mr. C. Southgate
Thron-EMI Information Technology Ltd.

Dr. K. Warren
Plessey Company plc.

Professor Eric Ash
University College London

Mr. R. Croft
DTI

Mr. C. Fielding
MoD

Mr. O. Roith
DTI

VLSI Program Coordinating Committee

Dr. W. Fawcett
Chairman, Alvey Directorate

Mr. M. Buck
Secretary, Alvey Directorate

Dr. M. O. Bryant
DCVD MoD (PE)

Mr. J. G. Noyes
DTI

Dr. D. E. Thomas
SERC

Dr. T. Walker
Alvey Directorage

Mr. R. F. Richards
CVD2 MoD (PE)

VLSI/CAD Industrial and Academic Committee

Mr. G. J. Lomer
Chairman, Racal Electronics

Mr. G. Adshead
ICL

Mr. D. Baker
BTRL

Dr. G. Dearnaley
AERE

Mr. J. S. Heeks
STL

Mr. W. Holt
Plessey Research

Dr. D. Hooper
GEC Hirst

Mr. I. Pearson
INMOS

Dr. G. F. Vanstone
Racal

Mr. R. Cutting
Sinclair

Dr. R. Hayes
Plessey

Professor H. Kemhadjian
Southampton University

Professor D. J. Kinniment
Newcastle University

General Circuit Devices Research Committee

R. G. Jones
Chairman, RSRE

Mr. M. Buck
Secretary, Alvey

Dr. T. I. Cox
RSRE

Mr. J. Vokes
CVD

Dr. T. E. Curtis
AUWE

Mr. D. C. Towers
CESG

Mr. R. F. Richards
CVD

Mr. B. R. Arthur
DTI

Dr. K. G. Barraclough
RSRE

Dr. V. I. G. Deshmukh
RSRE

Dr. J. P. Gillam
RSRE

Dr. J. R. Hill
RSRE

Dr. J. M. Keen
RSRE

Dr. J. C. White
RSRE

Dr. J. Woodward
RSRE

Mr. R. A. Lawes
RAL

Dr. D. Worsnip
SERC

Mr. W. Turner
RAL

Dr. D. J. Robbins
RSRE

Mr. J. G. Grimshaw
CVD

Computer Aided Design Committee

Dr. T. L. Thorp
Chairman, RSRE

Mr. R. F. Richards
MoD

Dr. D. R. S. Boyd
RAL

Dr. A. D. Bryden
RAL

Dr. J. A. McLean
RAL

Dr. D. Worsnip
SERC

Dr. C. O. Newton
RSRE

Dr. N. Peeling
RSRE

Dr. M. F. Boyer
RAE

Mr. G. C. Kingsley
GCHQ

Mr. D. Saunders
DTI

Mr. J. T. O'Conner
RARDE

Dr. G. Jones
RSRE

Mr. R. Aistrop
CVD

Mr. M. Newman
Alvey Directorate

Dr. R. Cripsin
Alvey Directorate

EARB Advanced Devices and Materials Committee

Mr. D. H. Roberts
Chairman, GEC

Dr. J. C. Bass
Plessey

Mr. R. W. Brander
BTRL

Mr. M. J. Coupland
STC

Dr. W. Fawcett
Alvey Directorate

Dr. K. W. Gray
RSRE

Mr. J. H. Major
DTI

Mr. J. G. Noyes
DTI

Dr. A. S. Shepherd
Ferranti

Mr. W. L. South
Philips

Mr. D. B. Thomas
Alvey Directorate and SERC

Mr. R. J. Franklin
DTI

Dr. J. R. Parks
DTI

Mr. R. R. Landeryou
DTI

Mr. F. C. Middleton
DTI

Computing and Communications Committee of EARB

P. J. A. Chandor
Chairman, MD Aregon International Ltd.

C. Haley
Technical Directorate ICL

P. Cohen
Logica VTS

R. K. Newman
Product Development Director OTL

D. Merlo
Deputy Directory Research BT

M. Sage
Southampton University

V. Stenning
Technical Director Imperial Software

J. Everard
MD Mitel Telecom

C. Jones
Manchester University

R. Needham
Cambridge University

B. Randell
Newcastle University

D. Tatham
CCTA

B. Gladman
MoD (RSRE)

D. Talbot
Alvey Directorate

Formal Methods Advisory Panel

Mr. M. I. Jackson
STL

Dr. H. Barringer
Manchester University

Mr. J. Elmore
BT

Professor C. A. R. Hoare
Oxford University

D. T. Maibaum
Imperial College

Mr. D. Morgan
Plessey Electronic Systems Research Ltd.

Dr. G. Plotkin
Edinburgh University

Dr. R. Snowdon
ICL

Mr. P. Sizer
Marconi Research Center

Professor C. B. Jones
Manchester University

Mr. S. Goodenough
RSRE

Mr. P. Dell
Acting Secretary, BT

Dr. R. Witty
Alvey Directorate

Reliability and Metrics Advisory Panel

Mr. N. Harris
Chairman, BAe

Dr. T. Anderson
Newcastle University

Mr. B. de Neumann
GEC

Ms. G. Frewin
STL

Mr. C. Gribble
Ferranti

Dr. B. Kitchener
ICL

Dr. B. Littlewood
City University

Mr. A. Wingrove
RAE

Mr. C. Dale
Secretary, UKAEA

IKBS Advisory Committee

Dr. J. A. N. Howe
Chairman, Edinburgh University

Dr. J. Fox
Imperial Cancer Research Fund

Professor R. Kowalski
Imperial College

Mr. M. Merry
Marconi Research

Dr. D. Probert
BT

Dr. T. O'Shea
Open University

Mr. G. Ricketts
Unilever

Dr. K. Sparck Jones
Cambridge University

Dr. J. Taylor
ASWE

Mr. R. Vaughn
SPL International

Dr. R. Worden
Logica

Dr. R. M. Young
Cambridge University

Alvey/SERC Special Interest Group in AI

Dr. A. C. Norman
Cambridge University

Mr. F. McCabe
Imperial College

Mr. J. Gibson
Sussex University

Dr. H. Thompson
Edinburgh University

Mr. J. Marks
Logica

Mr. C. Hughes
ICL

Mr. P. Sell
SPL

Mr. G. Waddinton
SDL

Mr. A. St. John
GEC Computers

Mr. S. Moralee
Unilever

Human Interface Proposal Appraisal Advisory Committee

Professor B. Shackel
Loughborough University

M. A. Knight
MoD Admiralty

Dr. M. Tainsh
MoD/APRE

Professor G. Colouris
Queen Mary College

Professor E. Edmonds
Leicester Polytechnic

C. W. Seager
DTI LA Division

A. Coates
SERC

Image Processing Proposal Appraisal Advisory Committee

Professor I. Alexander
Imperial College

Dr. A. Sleigh
RSRE

Dr. D. Rutovitz
Western General Hospital

Dr. C. Taylor
University of Manchester

R. A. Brook
SIRA

Dr. Balston
Plessey

A. Crowther
British Aerospace

G. Moss
DTI LA Division

A. Cotes
SERC

Demonstrators Advisory Committee

A. Burton
DTI/IT

A. C. Conway
DTI/LA

Dr. L. Goldstone
DTI/LA

P. J. Adkin
DTI/MEE

S. Owsianka
CCTA

D. Partridge
OSO

J. Williams
MoD

K. Bartlett
DTI/IT

A. Chandler
DHSS

Advisory Group For Alvey Network

Mr. F. Blake
NPL

Dr. D. Hartley
Alvey Directorate

Mr. J. Laws
RSRE

Dr. P. Linnington
RAL

Mr. J. Thomas
BT

Mr. K. Bartlett
ITSU

Professor M. Wells
JANET

Advisory Group On Information Services

Mr. D. L. A. Barber
Alvey Directorate

Mr. T. M. Aitchison
INSPEC

Mr. D. W. Harding
BCS

Dr. E. Laverick
IEE

Mr. G. J. Morris
ICL

Mr. P. W. Rivers-Latham
GEC

Mr. A. R. Terry
BARIC

Mrs. J. P. Tomlinson
IEE

CAM-I, Inc.
611 Ryan Plaza Dr.
Suite 1107
Arlington, TX 76011
(817) 860-1654
TWX: 910 890 5127 CAMI ARTN

William A. Carter
Sr. Vice President

Don Wechsler
Robotics Project Manager

John Forton

European Office:

CAM-I, Inc.
Newfoundland House
Poole Quay
Poole, Dorset
BH15 1HJ England
Telephone: (0202) 670717
TWX: 851 418 457 CAMI-G

Japan Representative:

Documentation and Engineering Corporation
c/o Shiba Mansion 205, 27-8
Shiba 2-chome, Minato-ku
Tokyo 105, Japan
TWX: 781 242 2093

T. Ikeda
President

Australian Office:

Swinburne Institute of Technology
P. O. Box 218
Hawthorne, Victoria 3122
Australia
Telephone: 03-819-8457
TWX: AA37769 SWINBN

James K. Russell
Head, Manufacturing Engineering Department

SYSTEM DEVELOPMENT FOUNDATION
Suite 210
181 Lytton Avenue
Palo Alto, CA 94301
(415) 328-5120